NORTHERN DANCER

NORTHERN DANCER

THE LEGEND AND HIS LEGACY

Muriel Lennox

MAINSTREAM
PUBLISHING

LONDON AND EDINBURGH

First published in Great Britain in 1999 by
MAINSTREAM PUBLISHING COMPANY (EDINBURGH) LTD
7 Albany Street
Edinburgh EH1 3UG

ISBN 1 84018 183 4

First published in Canada in 1995 by Beach House Books

A catalogue record for this book is available from the British Library

Typeset in Berkeley Book
Printed and bound in Great Britain by Butler & Tanner Ltd

For Philip

Contents

Preface

1 OCTOBER 1990
CHESAPEAKE BAY, MARYLAND, USA

Northern Dancer is standing several hundred yards away, in the centre of his paddock, his head lifted slightly. His ears are perked, his eyes focused on the horizon. He is standing still, which is curious: he was turned out in his paddock at sunrise and had been patrolling his domain the past seven hours, slowing only occasionally to grab a mouthful of grass. Now and then, when some far-off sound or movement caught his attention, he stopped briefly and sniffed the air, but then he was off again.

He stopped patrolling about one o'clock, when groom Bill Husfelt started leading the other stallions back to the barn for their afternoon meal. Northern Dancer calmly watched the procession, and hasn't moved in the half hour since.

Bill is leaning casually against the paddock gate, lead rope in hand. He has no intention of entering Northern Dancer's territory or challenging the stallion's legendary determination to do things his way. Bill was once savaged by a son of Northern Dancer's: he walked into The Minstrel's paddock to look for a halter and The Minstrel almost killed him. 'But then,' muses Bill, 'I was on his turf.' So he waits. And waits.

A red-tailed hawk drifts lazily overhead. The air is so still you can almost hear the wind rustling through its wing feathers. Periodically, mocking-birds gather on the barn roof to warble their repertoire of impersonations. Tiny yellow butterflies flitter and flutter.

Suddenly the silence is shattered by a piercing scream.

Now, only feet from the gate, Northern Dancer is up on his hind legs, hollering wildly. Bill is inside the paddock, keeping a cautious eye on the stallion's slashing front hooves. Northern Dancer slams his right hoof into the soft dirt with all his might. His nostrils are flaring, his eyes fierce.

Then once again he is standing perfectly still, his rib cage heaving from the exertion. When the stallion's breathing settles, Bill snaps the lead shank to his halter. Northern Dancer, it appears, has decided to go back to the barn.

His scream was so intense it resonated through my entire being. One second I was sitting on the grass daydreaming – the next my heart was pounding as if I had been physically assaulted.

When he was young, Northern Dancer could be extremely volatile. There was a scar in the shape of Northern Dancer's hoof on Harry Green's bald head – Harry hadn't got out of the way fast enough. But Northern Dancer is now 29, a very, very old horse – the life expectancy of thoroughbred stallions is about 22 years. For a horse his age to be rearing and hollering is as unlikely as an 80-year-old man to be pole-vaulting over his back fence into his neighbour's flower garden. Yet there he is – still wild as the wind.

When I arrived at the farm the previous day, Northern Dancer had been standing in the far corner of his spacious stall, his muzzle in the feed tub. The stall was bedded in fresh straw so deep it came almost to his knees and he seemed even smaller than I remembered.

Biographer I might be, but he was not curious – I was merely one of thousands who trek to Maryland to see him. Eventually he strolled over and gazed out through the bars of the stall. I gazed back. It was then that I wondered what I was going to do next. Had I driven all the way from Toronto just to stand outside his stall and stare at him?

I was having difficulty tracking down the people I had hoped to interview for this book while in Maryland, so I said to Bill in jest, 'Maybe I'll just interview Northern Dancer.' As I looked into the eyes of this remarkable animal I realised the question was not whether he could communicate, but whether I was capable of hearing. Sensing my quandary, Bill suggested I return the following morning, when Northern Dancer and the other stallions would be out in their paddocks.

So it was that since early morning I had been sitting, watching, waiting. A soft grey-blue mist hung over the gently rolling hills of Maryland's horse country, Cecil County. While the horses lounged in their fields, the rarely seen farm staff went about their chores quietly and calmly.

Each of the ten resident stallions had his own large grassy pasture, bordered by black four-board fences and separated by wide laneways. Northern Dancer's paddock was closest to the barn. When I got there he was grazing at the far end of his territory. He appeared much bigger, more powerful, than he had in his stall. Compared with the stallions in the surrounding paddocks – TV Commercial napped beneath a tree, others grazed lazily, and several did little but stand by the fence – Northern Dancer seemed even more energetic and intense.

There was something about his restless patrolling that gave one the sense of an animal in the wild guarding his territory, a feeling that to challenge him would prove dangerous. Ever on the alert, he behaved more like a wild stallion than a horse that had been pampered and fawned over all his life.

Around mid-morning I wandered down the lane beside his paddock, and eventually he deigned to come over to the fence. I cautiously tried patting him, but he warned me off: if I continued, he might be obliged to bite me.

What was a biographer to do? With no other option, I decided to interview him. I asked him about the Kentucky Derby, the Belmont. I told him about Nijinsky, The Minstrel, and the many great champions he had sired, that they had gone on to be sires and dams of great champions. I asked if he had any idea how all this had happened. I talked to him about his owner and breeder, E.P. Taylor, and Winifred, his wife, about how and when they had died.

Mrs Taylor had liked him right from the beginning. She would often walk over to the stables in the evening to visit him and bring him dinner mints. I believe they were kindred souls – both small in stature and enormous in spirit.

Throughout our interview, Northern Dancer stared at me. I thought he was listening, and the longer and deeper I looked into those large, intelligent eyes, the more he appeared to respond. He seemed sometimes curious, sometimes indifferent, but always alert. His were soft eyes, yet the fire still burned brightly. In my imagination another pair of eyes – E.P. Taylor's bright, blue ones –

smiled back at me. Taylor was the quintessential entrepreneur, yet of all his accomplishments, he would be remembered for this horse. I believe that would have pleased him.

I didn't realise there were tears rolling down my cheeks. This horse was such a big part of the Taylors' lives that he reminded me how much I missed them. Unconsciously I reached over, and this time Northern Dancer let me pat him. There was some mud caked by a patch of grey at his temple. The area between and below his nostrils, as soft as velvet on most horses, was as rough as sandpaper. When I started back up the lane he followed me on the other side of the fence.

He was in remarkably good shape, and showed only subtle signs of ageing. His back was slightly swayed and there was that bit of grey at his temples. His knees buckled a little from arthritis. Yet the muscles in his hind-quarters rippled and bulged. His stride was long and purposeful, his gait energetic.

When I went back to sit on the grass I discovered a four-leaf clover and had to smile. When Windfields had a horse entered in a big race, Mrs Taylor liked to tuck a four-leaf clover in her shoe. Most of us who lived on the Taylors' North Toronto estate would search the lawns and fields for one – we always found a four-leaf clover, even though the horse didn't always win.

I lived on the estate for 12 years as 'rider in residence': I kept E.P. Taylor's riding horses schooled and fit, and accompanied Taylor when he chose to ride, which he did frequently until he was almost eighty. I also worked with him on a number of projects, including the Jockey Club of Canada's inaugural graded-stakes programme, and lobbied the government for Ontario Jockey Club-controlled off-track betting. I also lobbied on my own behalf every time the Taylors flew to their Maryland farm and there was an empty seat on the company jet. I never wanted to miss an opportunity to visit Northern Dancer.

I love all horses, and none more than my own magical Philip, but I was always drawn to Northern Dancer. It wasn't until I finished writing this book that the magnetism began to make sense to me. I believe that the feeling took root deep in my soul 30 years ago when Northern Dancer won the Kentucky Derby. It wasn't just that he won; it was how he won that touched my heart.

Like so many others across Canada that first Saturday in May 1964, I was with a group of friends, gathered round the television to cheer on 'the Dancer'. During those thrilling final seconds of the race we jumped up and down, yelling, 'Come on, Dancer! Come on, Dancer!' as if he could hear us, as if our screaming would help him hold his oh-so-narrow lead.

When Northern Dancer won, we laughed, we cried. We hugged, we danced. And then we dropped, exhausted, on to chairs and sofas, grinning like imbeciles. You'd have thought we had run, and won, that race. But then, in a way we had. I believe that a part of each one of us ran with him that afternoon. Somewhere in the soul, his triumph became our triumph.

Had the saga of Northern Dancer ended there, with his Kentucky Derby victory, I would have been perfectly content. He was the little horse no one had wanted, had dismissed time after time – mostly because of his size. Yet, whatever Northern Dancer lacked in height, he more than made up for in heart. Still, no one could have predicted that as a sire, Northern Dancer would eclipse all other stallions in modern history. His dominance of thoroughbred racing and breeding the world over is unprecedented.

In 1993, the Epsom Derby, the Kentucky Derby, the Irish Derby, and the French Derby were won by great-grandsons of Northern Dancer. That autumn, 36 of the 88 élite entrants in the Breeders' Cup races were his direct descendants. In 1994 the number jumped to 56 of the 92 Breeders' Cup horses. So I wasn't long into this book before I realised that I had not only a story to tell, but also a mystery to explore. I found myself compelled to gain some insight into how Northern Dancer had come to be, and what it was that distinguished him from all the rest.

Tracing E.P. Taylor's role, I unearthed a hotchpotch of unrelated circumstances and curious situations that, when linked, led to Northern Dancer's being born in southern Ontario. Tracking Northern Dancer's brief career as a racehorse and the lead-up to the Derby left me with the impression that he was far more remarkable than had been credited: that he'd made it to Churchill Downs for the race was more extraordinary than his record-shattering victory.

My day watching and learning from Northern Dancer inspired me to observe the daily habits and rituals of other stallions, at Windfields and elsewhere. Many of them were sons of Northern Dancer. Some, like Danzig, were volatile; others, like Nijinsky, were highly intelligent. Vice Regent pranced and hollered down the path to the breeding arena. Little Lyphard, a physical replica of his sire, enjoyed getting his way, but was a gentler soul. Few would live to Northern Dancer's age, and none demonstrated the power and authority that Northern Dancer did that afternoon in Maryland. His savage stallion scream stayed with me throughout the four years it took to complete this book – a reminder, I suspect, for me to listen to him.

PART ONE
The Makings of a Legend

Northern Dancer must be regarded as one of the greatest, if not *the* greatest, sire of all time. It is incredible that such a small horse should have achieved so much success and carved such a niche for himself in the history of the thoroughbred.

Vincent O'Brien

Northern Dancer was the consequence of many factors. Some can be charted like an ancient treasure map; others can be analysed through genetic science. Yet, in the end, Northern Dancer is a celebration of life's mysteries, those things we cannot explain.

Perhaps the only thing more incredible than Northern Dancer's prominence is the story of how he came to be in the first place. The long road that led to this remarkable animal was marked with many twists and turns.

Central is the role played by E.P. Taylor, who as a young man became smitten by horses and thoroughbred racing. Year by year, his commitment to the sport intensified and, as it did, the vast stage upon which Northern Dancer would star came closer to becoming a reality.

For Northern Dancer was born of Taylor's dream that, contrary to popular opinion, great racehorses could be born and raised in Canada. While it is relatively simple, through selective matings, to produce a specific body type in an animal, the destiny of thoroughbreds is the racetrack. And it takes more than long legs and a perfectly sculpted body to win a race. Northern Dancer certainly proved that time and again. It takes heart: the will to win.

Little Northern Dancer had more of that elusive will to win than a herd of 40 horses. How did that happen?

Horse breeding is not unlike a poker game. Staying in the game means winning some, losing others. Sometimes beginner's luck, or dumb luck, prevails, however briefly. And every once in a long while, a royal flush in spades: a Northern Dancer appears.

One Man's Dream

Northern Dancer is in the winner's circle, tired, yet alert, with hundreds of tiny dark red roses, woven into a blanket, draped across his withers. The track announcer declares that Northern Dancer's new Kentucky Derby record is official: two minutes flat. Faster than Citation, Whirlaway, Swaps, Count Fleet, War Admiral – all the American turf legends.

The hundred thousand Derby fans respond to the announcement with thunderous applause. Northern Dancer's small ears flick back and forth as he adjusts to the roar of the crowd. Never has the colt experienced so much noise. Patting Northern Dancer's sweaty neck is his proud owner, E.P. Taylor. Behind his horn-rimmed glasses, Taylor's eyes sparkle. 'This is a great day for Canada!' he declares.

It is also a great day for the 63-year-old Taylor – the fulfilment of a dream he had been pursuing for 45 years, a dream most people believed impossible. Years earlier A.B. 'Bull' Hancock, owner of Claiborne Farm, the most successful thoroughbred breeding farm in the US at mid-century, had advised Taylor that if he wanted to make money with his horses he should 'stay in Canada, forget Kentucky'.

'Dad told me that Bull and some of his other Kentucky friends used to tell him in the '50s that he'd never breed a good horse in Canada,' recalled Charles Taylor. 'All that snow and ice.'

To the Kentuckians on their grand blue-grass stud farms, raising a good horse, much less a champion, in Canada was about as likely as growing palm trees on Baffin Island. They had a point. Horses are by nature grazing animals, and thrive when free to roam pasture lands. The grasses that flourish in Kentucky's temperate climate and mineral-rich soil provide an excellent environment for raising thoroughbreds, and thus Kentucky is recognised as the hub of the thoroughbred breeding business in North America. The majority of the leading US thoroughbreds have been born and raised in Kentucky. Until Northern Dancer, none had come from Canada. The mere idea of young thoroughbreds cavorting in paddocks of snow up to their bellies as Arctic winds whipped across the open fields would have made a Kentuckian blanch.

E.P. Taylor thrived on challenges. 'I would have done better financially if I had stuck to one enterprise,' he confided one afternoon, 'but having a variety of challenges was more appealing.' He would also have had more money had he not spent millions on his horses. He was a visionary and a born promoter, yet his prominence as a powerful businessman masked his often eccentric nature. He was a force unto himself, and if it were at all possible to produce a champion thoroughbred in Canada, or to grow palm trees on Baffin Island, E.P. Taylor would find a way.

The impossible dream that culminated in Northern Dancer began on 10 May 1919, when Montreal, Quebec, briefly experienced a great enthusiasm for thoroughbred racing. The catalyst was a rangy chestnut colt called Sir Barton. Owned by Montreal sportsman J.K.L. Ross, although bred in Kentucky, Sir Barton won the 1919 Kentucky Derby; Ross's other horse, Billy Kelly, finished second. The excitement in Ross's home town escalated when Sir Barton went on to capture both the Preakness and the Belmont, and thus became the first US Triple Crown winner.

Just months prior to all this excitement, young Edward Taylor had arrived in Montreal from Ottawa to pursue a degree in mechanical engineering at McGill University. For him, horses were merely sturdy animals that clattered along Ottawa's streets hauling delivery wagons. But the summer Sir Barton triumphed was also the summer Edward Taylor discovered racing. Every weekend he caught the streetcar that rattled up to Bluebonnets, or the ferry across the river to King Edward Park on Ile Gros Bois. He was smitten.

One morning during his first year at McGill he was toasting a piece of bread when he came up with the idea that provided the seed money for his involvement in thoroughbred racing. At the time, toasters toasted only one side of a piece of bread. Turning over the bread was a ridiculous waste of time, decided the impatient 17-year-old Taylor. Obviously the world needed a toaster that would do both sides at once. So he built one. He patented his invention and sold it to a Montreal firm in exchange for a royalty on every household toaster sold. He also talked them into giving him a summer job, which helped pay his tuition and living expenses. The royalties from the toaster funded his frequent excursions to Montreal's racetracks.

Taylor graduated from McGill with a degree in mechanical engineering and a passion for horses. He never practised as an engineer, not even one day – but horses, particularly thoroughbreds, remained the focus of his life. Since there was no thoroughbred racing of consequence in Ottawa, he decided to gain a different perspective on horses. After a few lessons at the local riding school, he joined the Princess Louise Dragoon Guards, a ceremonial cavalry regiment. His first outing with the Guards was a 14-mile trek through the streets of Ottawa. When a streetcar rattled past the mounted troop, the inexperienced Taylor could not control his horse. The animal bolted up the steps of a nearby Catholic church.

'If the door had been open,' Taylor said with a chuckle at the memory, 'I'm certain the horse would have gone right up to the altar.' Undaunted, he became an adept rider and rode at every opportunity. He would frequently arrive for business meetings at his office on his estate on horseback. One such morning his horse, a lanky grey thoroughbred gelding, came back alone.

'When I saw that horse I thought, Oh, geez, what's happened to the boss?' recalled stallion manager Harry Green. 'When we found Mr Taylor, he was on the ground, unable to move. He was way over there on the other side of the river. No trucks could get through, so we hitched up a hay wagon to one of the big tractors. And that's how we got him home.'

He had fractured his pelvis. His doctor warned him never to ride again as a subsequent accident might cripple him for life. But he continued to ride for almost thirty more years. He truly loved being on the back of a horse, loved a good gallop. And he loved the animal itself. More than once I caught a glimpse of him in a stall talking to his horse, his arms affectionately around its neck.

Winifred Taylor shared her husband's passion for horses – from a distance. When invited to join a ride at Windfields she demurred. 'I'd love to, dear,' she'd say, 'but I'm terribly afraid my riding breeches are at the dry cleaner's.' Her sport was tennis. One of their early dates, a Saturday afternoon at Ottawa's Connaught Park Racetrack, was Winifred Duguid's first visit to a thoroughbred meet. By the end of the day, Taylor had wagered and lost all the money in his wallet.

'I was very sorry,' Mrs Taylor said years later. 'The races were such fun, but I thought when Eddie lost all his money, he'd not ever want to go racing again.' She need not have worried.

E.P. Taylor's engineering degree languished, surpassed by his desire to engineer business deals. Before he was 30 he had started up and sold a bus company, then a taxi company; worked his way from bond salesman to partner in the brokerage firm McLeod, Young, Weir; and incorporated the Brewing Corporation of Ontario, the cornerstone of his business philosophy and wealth, which would also play a important part in the creation of Northern Dancer.

Taylor's father, a colonel in the Canadian army, was stationed in England during World War I. The colonel had his family with him, but 15-year-old Edward ran off time and again to join the British army. Finally the exasperated colonel shipped Edward back home to live with his maternal grandfather, Charles Magee. A successful entrepreneur who dabbled in everything from dry-goods to banking to breweries, Magee spent the next year teaching his young grandson the intricacies of corporate dealmaking. Magee died during the summer of 1918, just before young Edward went to university, but his influence was enormous. 'My ambition was to do the same kind of things he did,' Taylor later said.

Magee was the majority shareholder in a small Ottawa brewery called Brading's, and when young Edward returned home after university he was appointed a director of the company. Following the repeal of the Temperance Act in 1927, he presented the directors with an idea for major expansion. They said no. Undaunted, he decided instead, in the wake of the 1929 stock-market crash, to revamp the entire brewing industry of Ontario.

There were almost forty breweries scattered throughout Ontario; one large operation, he reasoned, would function more efficiently, and he set out to convince the owners of the small breweries. Since he had nowhere near the amount of money needed to buy out the breweries, he offered the owners shares in his proposed holding company, the Brewing Corporation of Ontario. Then he learned that an American promoter, Clarke Jennison, had a similar idea. He also had half a million dollars raised from British investors. In March 1930, the Brewing Corporation of Ontario was incorporated, with E.P. Taylor as president and general manager and C.S. Jennison as chairman. Within a year they had acquired ten breweries.

In the spring of 1936, Taylor decided to merge his beer interests with his passion for thoroughbreds. By law – a carryover from the days of prohibition – he was not allowed to advertise his beer. He could, however, advertise a racing stable, even if it just happened to share the name Cosgrave with one of his brands of beer.

On 25 April 1936, he hired a colourful character named Bert Alexandra to be his trainer, explaining that he wanted to build a large racing stable with virtually no money. He eventually came up with somewhere between $3,600 and $7,500 – in later years Taylor and Alexandra couldn't agree on the exact amount – which the wily Alexandra used to purchase a small herd of horses. The Cosgrave racing stable was up and running.

One of the Cosgrave horses was an exceptional filly called Mona Bell. Soon coloured prints of Mona Bell adorned the walls of every beer parlour in southern Ontario. Beneath the picture of the proud filly was the name COSGRAVE.

Taylor's plan worked well: the stable prospered and publicity was indirectly generated for Cosgrave beer. Starting up Cosgrave was extremely significant, not only for the evolution of Northern Dancer, but for thoroughbred racing in general. It took Taylor from the reasonably maintained stands of the various racetracks, into the ghetto-like living conditions endured by both horses and handlers in the backstretch.

In 1947, Taylor accepted an invitation to become a member of the Ontario Jockey Club. Thoroughbred racing in Canada would never be the same. There were seven tracks within eighty miles of Toronto, but all were limping along under a federal law that allowed only 14 racing days a year for each track.

'I was actually afraid that racing here would die right out,' recalled Taylor. 'The tracks and stabling were in very bad shape. The buildings were falling down and could easily have been labelled firetraps.'

Jim Coleman, syndicated columnist with Southern Newspapers,

named it 'the leaky roof circuit'. And that it was. The first thing grooms did when they arrived at a track was try to find a stall dry enough to sleep in. Then they'd scurry about looking for decent shelter for their horses. At Fort Erie the grooms were offered all they could eat for 35 cents – a good deal if they could fight off the flies.

Chicanery was rampant at all the tracks. Jockeys, trainers, and mobsters were linked in sometimes subtle, often blatant, race fixing. Horses were run on all kinds of drugs, including heroin. 'Something had to be done to improve those conditions,' Taylor said. 'So I did it. Someone had to.'

Taylor approached thoroughbred racing with the same enthusiasm that he had shown when taking on the brewing industry. Soon he was the largest shareholder in the Ontario Jockey Club, the proprietors of Woodbine Racetrack (later called Greenwood), on the shores of Lake Ontario. By the end of 1952, under Taylor's direction the Ontario Jockey Club had bought all the tracks. Taylor sold off all but two and set out to build the most modern racetrack in the world.

New Woodbine was officially opened on 12 June 1956, 20 years after Taylor had commissioned Bert Alexandra to begin the Cosgrave Stable. During that time he had single-handedly rescued Canadian racing and recreated it in his own image.

The chain of events leading to Northern Dancer began when the phone rang in Taylor's office in the autumn of 1950. It was Colonel R.S. 'Sam' MacLaughlin, an avid horseman and founder of Canada's motor industry. He explained to Taylor that because he was nearing his eightieth birthday, he had arrived at the difficult decision to sell Parkwood Stables, his 470-acre horse farm north of Oshawa, Ontario. He had received a substantial offer from a real-estate developer, but he loved Parkwood dearly and was prepared to take much less for it if the buyer kept it as a horse farm. He asked Taylor if he knew anyone who might be interested.

Taylor didn't. The owners of the major Canadian racing stables already had their own farms, and he himself had spent a great deal of money building the large red brick stables, with their miles of white board fences, adjacent to his Bayview Avenue home in Toronto. Indeed, Windfields Farm was a showpiece.

And then François Dupré came to town. The owner of a stud farm in Normandy, France, who from time to time ran horses in Canada, he was immediately interested in Parkwood. Taylor quickly arranged a meeting with Colonel Sam, but by the time their lunch took place Dupré had changed his mind. Taylor was now becoming as anxious as Colonel Sam that the lovely old farm be spared. When lunch was over he said to him, 'Give me 48 hours. I think I can find a solution.'

Taylor was on the phone for the next two days, canvassing friends, thoroughbred owners, and business associates. His idea was to turn Parkwood into a breeding farm similar to the National Stud in England. Its sole purpose would be to raise the quality of Canadian thoroughbreds. By the deadline he had commitments from nine men, who, with Taylor, would each hold a 10 per cent interest in the operation. He called Colonel Sam, told him of his plan, and made an offer to buy Parkwood. Colonel Sam was delighted and accepted immediately.

In the transaction Colonel Sam excluded nothing on the farm except his riding horse, several racehorses, and about eighty very fat cattle. Eventually the cattle were included in the deal.

Parkwood was a grand and graceful estate. A long, tree-lined lane led to the heart of property. The cream-coloured stuccoed walls of the giant riding arena, barns, and stables were trimmed with hunter green, as were the doors and rows of window frames; and the paddock fences were painted black. Although Parkwood was imposing in its elegance, it blended subtly with the landscape.

Once the deal was about to close, Taylor had second thoughts. He went back over the financial implications of creating his proposed National Stud Farm and realised that initial losses would be staggering. He immediately called his nine partners and told them they were off the hook. Instead he bought the farm on his own!

Taylor was a shrewd businessman, and such impulsive decision-making was completely out of character. Furthermore, there was no money to be had in breeding thoroughbreds, especially in Canada. Men like Taylor built their farms strictly as a place to house their own horses. Horses were their hobby, an expensive hobby, even for people of Taylor's considerable wealth. It would be a long time before stallions were syndicated for megamillions, before yearlings were sold for hundreds of thousands, before breeding thoroughbreds was big business.

Taylor's Windfields started as a small four-horse stable. By the time he bought Parkwood, Windfields Farm had expanded to accommodate a herd of almost a hundred horses: two stallions, thirty-four brood mares, yearlings, foals, and racing and riding horses. If Parkwood had not come on the market, and Taylor had not rushed into buying, it's unlikely he would have pursued the idea of breeding a champion capable of winning classic races. At the time, he was involved in scores of business enterprises in the United States, Great Britain, and across Canada. He was hardly looking for something to occupy his time, energy and money.

Once he made a commitment, however, he never looked back, even though experience told him that everything cost more, took longer, and was much more challenging than he had thought in the beginning. Buoyed by an unwavering faith in his ability to sell whatever it was he had created, he simply refused to quit.

Once the deed to Parkwood was in his hands, he held a dispersal of all the cattle and horses except the stallions. He changed the name of the farm to the National Stud Farm and he hired the best available horsemen to run the operation. He talked Gil Darlington, a respected authority on thoroughbred breeding, into leaving his own Trafalgar Farm in Oakville, Ontario, to act as general manager. Gil brought in Peter Poole, a young horseman from British Columbia, to be his assistant and persuaded Taylor to hire Pete McCann, the brilliant and bashful trainer, to replace Bert Alexandra.

Bert had decided to take early retirement and, in retrospect, it was the appropriate time for Taylor and him to go their separate ways. Straight out of the pages of Damon Runyon, Bert Alexandra wasn't above a bit of mischief, taking an edge in a race, which, he believed, was his job as a trainer. Racing was about to change radically, and at the hands of his employer. Bert knew it wouldn't be as much fun any more, nor would he fit the new mould. When I asked Taylor about Bert years later and mentioned the wonderful, often outrageous stories he told about 'the good old days', Taylor's response was, 'You can't put any trust in what a man who doesn't work has to say.'

Mrs Taylor, however, adored Bert, and never tired of his endless yarns. Her nickname for him was 'The Gypsy'. One evening at dinner she confided to me, 'I know Eddie had to change racing – things, especially for the horses, were very bad. But I do sometimes miss the old days. We had such fun. It's a much more serious business now.'

Taylor plucked the fourth member of the National Stud's

management team from Windfields. Harry Green, a horse-van driver for the local veterinary as soon as his feet could reach the pedals in the old truck, had been looking after the stallions on Taylor's farm. Harry would now take charge of the stallions at the National Stud.

At the first management meeting Taylor revealed his plan to make the farm pay for itself while upgrading the quality of Canadian thoroughbreds: 'It will be the stakes winners at the racetrack that will actually make this farm for us.' Successful racehorses would be the advertising campaign; although the farm might lose money on the racehorses, they would more than make it up in breeding. Optimistically, he offered thoroughbred owners a complete range of facilities for breeding, foaling, raising, and training at a reasonable price. As an additional incentive he reduced the stud fees of the five stallions standing at the farm.

But this was the fall of 1950, and although people such as Taylor continued to raise and race their horses, the sport and the tracks were on the brink of collapse. The purses were so low that $1,500 was considered top purchase price for a horse. Buying Parkwood certainly enhanced Taylor's commitment to thoroughbred racing, and two years later he began, through the Ontario Jockey Club, to buy up all the Ontario tracks and rebuild the sport. For the National Stud Farm to become economically viable, however, it would have to produce horses capable of winning lucrative US stakes races. And so it was that Taylor set his sights on the Kentucky Derby.

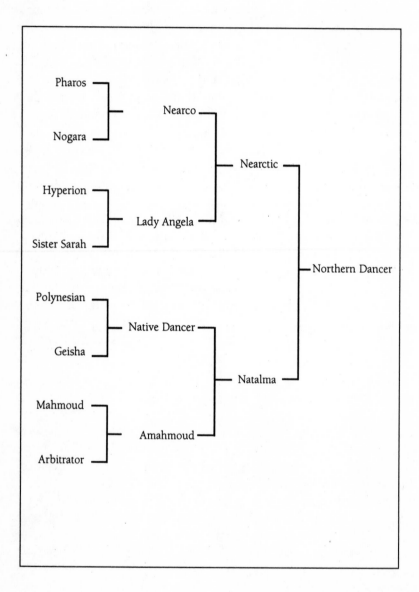

Echoes of Distant Ancestors

There can be little doubt that from his extraordinary nature to his extreme prepotency, Northern Dancer was a phenomenon. On one level, rare and exceptional beings just appear. Yet they are the consequence of genetic data and incidental events that on their own appear to be unrelated fragments of the past. Only when the pieces fit together does the portrait emerge. Northern Dancer may well have been the embodiment of the very best traits of his ancestors.

Galton's Law of Hereditary Influence states that 50 per cent of an individual's inherited characteristics comes from its parents. Each set of grandparents contributes 12.5 per cent, and so on in a declining mathematical progression. Each characteristic requires two genes, one from each parent. A gene is either dominant, in which case it appears in the individual, or recessive, in which case it lies dormant from one generation to the next, until, given the right circumstances, it is expressed. Could it be that recessive genes combined to create this super-horse? While a genetic analysis of Northern Dancer would prove mere speculation, a trip through his genealogy suggests he may have emerged from very special qualities of distant, long-forgotten ancestors.

E.P. Taylor didn't set out to prove that it was possible to raise a horse in Canada that would change the destiny of thoroughbreds the world over. He was simply hoping for a horse capable of winning the Kentucky Derby. To achieve the ideal of an animal blessed with the stamina, speed, heart and determination to win classic races, Taylor reasoned that he would have to invest in the best bloodlines. There's an axiom in the inexact science of breeding thoroughbreds: 'If you want the best, breed the best to the best, and hope for the best.'

Taylor decided to go straight to the source: Newmarket, England, the heartland of British racing. He contracted George Blackwell, a young representative with the British Bloodstock Agency, to purchase the finest brood mare offered at the 1952 December Sales at Newmarket. Money was to be no object. Selecting the mare was the simplest part of George's first commission for this new Canadian client. 'It was really no problem,' recalled Blackwell. 'Lady Angela was by far the best mare in the sale.' She was eight years old, and both her dam and sire traced back to some of the most outstanding horses in British racing history. And she was in foal to the great champion Nearco.

'I contacted Taylor, and he agreed immediately, except for one thing,' Blackwell continued. 'He wanted her to remain in England, have her foal, then be bred back again to Nearco.'

Blackwell immediately approached Lady Angela's owner, Martin Benson (coincidentally the majority shareholder in Nearco), with Taylor's proposal. Benson refused, offering no explanation. He may have been reluctant to use his breeding rights to Nearco on any mare other than his own. Blackwell relayed Benson's adamant refusal to Taylor.

'He told me quite emphatically that those were his terms. And that if I was unable to secure a return breeding, he was no longer interested in the mare,' said Blackwell. 'So I called Martin Benson once again. Eventually, and I must say reluctantly, he agreed to see me again. He continued to be quite firmly opposed to the idea. Finally I told him that this client was a very wealthy Canadian and that his co-operation in this arrangement might be good for future horse sales.' Benson wavered, but was not convinced. He said he'd think about it.

The deciding factor turned out to be Britain's currency controls. Benson, a wealthy British bookmaker, sought refuge in Florida from England's cold, damp winters. The amount of money he was allowed to take on his annual vacation, however, was severely limited. He contacted Blackwell and said that he would agree to the return breeding to Nearco if Taylor supplied him with $3,000 in American currency on Benson's next Florida vacation.

Taylor agreed to the terms and Blackwell went to the Newmarket sale. The bidding on Lady Angela rocketed to $35,000 before

Blackwell secured the mare for Taylor. In the early 1950s this was a colossal sum to pay for a mare – albeit one with a fine family tree – who had distinguished herself neither as a racehorse nor as a dam of racehorses. Following the sale, Lady Angela returned to Benson's Beech House Stud to foal and be bred back to Nearco, and Martin Benson wintered in Florida with his additional spending money. Taylor optimistically named the foal Empire Day, for the Canadian national holiday celebrating Queen Victoria's birthday. As a racehorse, Empire Day gave his owners little cause to celebrate. He started thirty-six times and won three minor events. The foal from the return breeding was Nearctic, sire of Northern Dancer.

Why did Taylor insist on breeding Lady Angela once again to Nearco? It simply was not logical. Nearco and Hyperion, sire of Lady Angela, were the pre-eminent stallions in England at the time. Hyperion sired particularly outstanding brood mares. Almost every British Hyperion mare had been bred to Nearco again and again. Yet, other than Noory, the 1952 Irish Oaks winner, nothing suggested this breeding formula had any merit.

Moreover, Lady Angela already had two foals by Nearco, neither of which was inclined to be a racehorse. The first was a temperamental filly called Mary Martin, the other a colt called Gabriel. If her owners named him after the archangel herald of good news, their faith must have been sorely tested. He won only one minor race. (He had been gelded early on, which suggests he may have been difficult to handle.) These discouraging results were, no doubt, why Martin Benson decided to sell the mare. Lady Angela was ridden to the post seven times, but won only the August Plate, a maiden three-year-old, mile-long race at Epsom. Shortly thereafter she was retired to Benson's Newmarket farm.

Benson must have held great hope for her as a brood mare, since Lady Angela came from a long line of prolific mares that produced countless stakes winners. Four generations back was Pretty Polly, the sensational racemare that at the turn of the century won an amazing 22 of her 24 starts, including the English Oaks and the St Leger. Although Pretty Polly's six sons were not notable, her four daughters were all winners, and each established her own successful family line. Lady Angela's connection was through the powerful Molly Desmond branch of the Pretty Polly matriarchal dynasty.

Although stallions get most of the attention in this generally patriarchal sport, it is widely held that the mares dominate the genetic inheritance of the offspring, and by as much as 70 to 75 per cent. So, through Lady Angela, Northern Dancer may well have inherited genes not only from this dynamic female line, but also that of her sire, the acclaimed champion racehorse and sire of exceptional brood mares, Hyperion.

Northern Dancer certainly shared the height – or lack of it – of his maternal grandsire. When Hyperion reached maturity he measured fifteen hands one and a half inches, a half inch shorter than Northern Dancer. (One hand equals four inches and is measured from the bottom of the front hoof to the withers at the base of the neck above the shoulders.)

Hyperion was so tiny at birth that the stable lads joked that he looked more like a golden retriever than a horse. Chilling winds whipped across Lord Derby's Woodlands Stud stable yard that cold and grey Good Friday in 1930. When Lady Derby saw the little golden chestnut colt with four white socks lying in the stall beside his dam, Selene, she suggested he be named Hyperion, after the Titan father of the sun god of Greek mythology.

In the spring of 1932, as Hyperion was about to make his racing debut, he was a mere fourteen hands two inches (four feet ten inches), the size of a child's pony; he was, however, perfectly proportioned. Hyperion's size should not have come as a surprise. His dam, Selene, was so small that Lord Derby's trainer, George Lambton, felt there was no point in nominating her to Britain's classic races; yet Selene sped to 16 victories and was never out of the money. Unfortunately Lambton's hasty judgement disallowed her from contesting the classics; by the time he realised she was a champion, the nominations were closed.

Selene's sire, Chaucer, wasn't much bigger than a pony, and Chaucer's dam, Canterbury Pilgrim, was much the same size as Hyperion. Not only was little Selene an outstanding racehorse, she was possibly the pre-eminent brood mare in history, the matriarch of an international dynasty of champions. She was the great-great-grandam to many US legends: Native Dancer (Sickle – Unbreakable – Polynesian – Native Dancer); Buckpasser (Pharmond – Menow – Tom Fool – Buckpasser); Kelso (Hyperion – Alibhai – Your Host – Kelso). Many top South American thoroughbreds trace their lineage back to Selene through another of her offspring, the stallion

Hunter's Moon. Her most notable son, however, both as a stallion and a racehorse, was little Hyperion.

Yet no one witnessing Hyperion enter training would have predicted he was destined for glory. He showed absolutely no inclination to race. While the other young horses leaped, snorted, and jogged over Newmarket Heath in the fresh morning air, eager to stretch their limbs in a good gallop, Hyperion was content to amble along, in no way affected by their antics. After riding him in several training gallops, Tommy Weston opined that Hyperion was either 'dead lazy or next to useless'. During these outings Hyperion would come to a complete halt without warning, whenever and wherever the notion struck him.

Five years after his death at 29, workers discovered, when assembling his skeleton to display in a museum, that he possessed an extra pair of ribs, inherited from his distant Arab ancestors, and a thickening of the hyoid bone, by his left ear. It was suggested that Hyperion might have suffered some degree of deafness, which would account for his stopping to peruse the countryside while the pack galloped on. Flight animals by nature and design, horses have extremely sensitive hearing that allows them to detect impending danger miles away. If Hyperion did indeed have a hearing problem, his stopping may have had something to do with an inability to perceive sounds accurately at a distance.

Hyperion had a curious fascination with birds. If a hawk swooped into a hedgerow he raced across the field to check on its landing. During the war he was shipped to Yorkshire, where he spent long hours observing pheasants scooting in and out of the shrubs in a far corner of his pasture. He'd wait until a number of the big birds gathered, before trotting over to take a closer look and frighten them back into the air. When he returned to Newmarket his fascination became aeroplanes: once he spotted one, he focused on it to the exclusion of all else, until it disappeared. This is very unusual behaviour. In *Breeding the Racehorse*, Federico Tesio concludes that thoroughbreds are unable to distinguish objects further than 150 yards, and horses by virtue of their anatomy have 'considerable difficulty looking upwards'. They have peripheral vision that allows them an almost 360-degree panorama when grazing. They also have bifocal vision, in order to see the grass beneath their teeth and into the distance. They aren't hunters and therefore don't need the eyesight of a hawk, and they depend on their other highly developed senses to alert them to danger.

In a note to Lord Derby in the spring of 1932, George Lambton wrote: 'The two-year-olds are backward, Hyperion particularly so.' Yet he was not about to make the same mistake with Hyperion as he had with Selene, and thus posted nomination fees to the classic races on behalf of the little colt. When Hyperion was shipped to Doncaster for his first race, however, Lambton didn't go; instead he sent jockey Tommy Weston, with instructions not to finish last and not to use his whip.

The five-furlong Zetland Plate lured nineteen starters that grey and drizzly Yorkshire afternoon. The bookmakers shared the general lack of faith in Hyperion's ability and lumped him in with a dozen 'others' at 25–1 odds.

Until the race Hyperion had experienced nothing but the tranquil countryside around Newmarket. The first exposure to the noise and frenetic energy of a racecourse is unnerving to most horses. Not so Hyperion. The carnival atmosphere, the chatter of the bookmakers, the whoops and yells as the horses pounded closer and closer to the post seemed to ignite something inside Hyperion: he cantered down to the start, his ears perked, his bright eyes shining. Quite conceivably Hyperion's change of attitude was due to the clamour, which may have allowed him to hear well for the first time.

About halfway down the straight, Tommy Weston gave Hyperion a tap on the shoulder with his whip, just to ensure they didn't finish last. Hyperion bolted forward so quickly Weston had to scramble to stay in the saddle. Hyperion finished a fast-closing fourth. After the race Weston confessed that had he known Hyperion was a race-horse he would have ridden him differently, and they'd have won by several lengths.

When he returned home to Newmarket, Hyperion reverted to his old nonchalant self. Indeed, throughout his spectacular racing career he showed complete indifference to training gallops. Yet on the racecourse he became fired with energy and blistering speed, as he carried the famous Derby racing colours – black shirt with one white button and white cap – to victory in Britain's classic races, including the St Leger, the Prince of Wales's Stakes and the Epsom Derby.

Hyperion was not only the smallest Derby winner since Little Wonder, in 1840, but the fastest. He flew past the finishing post in a record two minutes thirty-four seconds. (Three years later the Aga Khan's Mahmoud was clocked at 2:33.8, but because the races were timed with stop watches, the accuracy was considered susceptible to human frailty.)

'Hyperion was a great racehorse, a great sire and a great sire of brood mares,' wrote Lord Derby in the Foreword to *Hyperion*, 'but above all else he was a great character, and that's how I will always remember him.'

Among the many prominent daughters of Hyperion was Hydroplane II, dam of the US legend Citation. It seemed therefore reasonable to assume that breeding Nearco to a daughter of Hyperion would produce yet another great champion. But the blood and genes of these two great horses simply didn't mix. True, this combination yielded some runners, and two stakes winners. Yet only once did this mixture really take fire, when Taylor insisted that Lady Angela be bred, once more, to Nearco. But then, Nearco too was born of curious fate.

Northern Dancer's paternal grandsire surely was proof of the adage 'when your best-laid plans go absolutely wrong, beware, something quite remarkable might happen'.

Federico Tesio is duly celebrated as the breeder of Nearco. Yet if things had gone according to Tesio's plan, Nearco would not have been born. Respected as one of the world's foremost authorities on breeding thoroughbreds, Tesio – in appearance, character, and methodology – was much like Agatha Christie's Hercule Poirot. Tesio's inquiring mind was orderly and shrewd, and his observations on the nature of horses in *Breeding the Racehorse* are fundamental to any study of equine behaviour. When selecting mates for his small herd of mares, Tesio carefully examined every possible detail, from the potential effects of the mare's long journey from his Dormello Stud in northern Italy to the physical attributes, failings, character, and peculiarities of the stallion and his forebears. He even examined the layout of the farm and, of course, the competence of the staff.

When choosing a stallion for Nogara, the former Italian cavalry officer was even more thorough than usual. Nogara was one of Tesio's favourites. Her conformation, small and compact, was ideal in Tesio's opinion. After considerable deliberation, Tesio finally settled on Lord Derby's Fairway as the perfect mate for Nogara. The two animals complemented each other in every way, from physique to disposition. Nogara had won several Italian classic races, but her maximum distance was a mile and a quarter; Fairway had won the St Leger at almost two miles.

It appears Tesio pondered too long over the details of this potential mating. By the time he contacted Lord Derby's stud manager, Fairway's book was full. In despair, Tesio reluctantly decided to send Nogara to France to be bred to Fairway's full brother, Pharos. Compact and muscular, Pharos was the physical opposite of Fairway, and had not proven himself to be a distance horse. Tesio held no hope for the mating.

On 24 January 1935, he apparently showed no interest in Nogara's newborn foal. But several months later Tesio conducted an experiment that grew out of his observations several decades earlier, and Nogara's little colt, Nearco, was part of the experiment.

In the early 1900s, Tesio had come upon a herd of nearly 20,000 migrating bison on the Canadian prairies. It was autumn and the bison were moving south towards their winter grazing grounds. How did they know where to go or when? Tesio reasoned that all beings have a sixth sense that guides them to whatever it is they crave or need for survival. This sixth sense picks up radiations or vibrations emitted by the object or destination, regardless of distance or obstacles. Vibrations emanating from the winter pasture, Tesio concluded, were picked up by the bisons' intuitive guidance system.

When he returned to Italy, Tesio noticed that each autumn, as the brood mares were turned out on to a new pasture, they slowly moved across the field, stripping it bare in a fortnight. As winter approached, the mares dug in the ground with their hooves to get at the grass roots. Finally, they stood anxiously along the fence at the southern end of the paddock. Like the bison, Tesio believed the mares were picking up signals that would guide them to winter pasture: if the mares had been on their own they would instinctively have journeyed south.

So Tesio decided to try an experiment. In the autumn of 1935 and each year thereafter, he shipped all his weanlings south to spend the winter grazing and growing at Oligiata, the estate of the Marchese Incisa. There is nothing to indicate whether this experiment was a success, except, perhaps, that three exceptional animals, Donatello, Ribot, and Nearco, were participants.

Some would call the weanling Nearco a bully, some a born leader, but running free in the paddock at Oligiata, Nearco constantly harassed the others. He would trot up to one of the colts and give him a shove with his shoulder, like a body check in ice hockey. Stocky and strong, Nearco invariably sent his victim staggering. Nearco's aggressiveness convinced Tesio that he could make something of this colt, who was blossoming into a beautiful, symmetrically proportioned horse. He had speed to spare. No matter what Tesio asked of him, no matter what weight Tesio had him carry, Nearco did it with ease, even indifference.

Tesio was fanatical about training. He believed that a horse should race only if it was at peak fitness: it was preferable to lose a race because of overconditioning than underconditioning. In the latter, he was convinced, the horse not only risked injury, but might be turned off racing entirely.

Tesio's unusual training methods were gruelling, and because of Nearco's superiority – and no doubt his indifference – Tesio worked the colt even harder than the others. Yet in morning gallops and in races, Nearco did exactly what was asked of him. Neither bad-tempered nor difficult, he was unflinching. At the sound of the starter's pistol Nearco simply galloped off and won without taking notice of the other horses in the race.

The final event in Nearco's brilliant career was the nearly two-mile Grand Prix de Paris on Sunday, 26 June 1938, at Longchamps. He left the rest of the field, including the French and British Derby winners, far behind and was heralded Champion of Europe.

With war looming over Europe, less than a week later Tesio sold Nearco to Martin Benson for £60,000, then the highest price paid for a thoroughbred. Nearco was shipped immediately to England to stand at Benson's Beech House Stud near Newmarket. When air-raids menaced Newmarket, Nearco and his groom moved to Wales, where they stayed for two months. As the bombing moved towards the coast of Wales, however, they returned to Newmarket, where a special air-raid shelter was constructed for Nearco in his paddock.

Nearco sired many top racehorses, including English Derby winners Dante and Nimbus, as well as a number of prominent stallions. In North America two of his sons created dynamic new bloodlines: Nasrullah, sire of Bold Ruler and grandsire of Secretariat, and forebear of many great US champions; and Nearctic, sire of Northern Dancer.

Beating the Odds

Northern Dancer's sire, Nearctic, was the result of E.P. Taylor's faith in what was presumed to be a failed formula, but Taylor's bartering with Martin Benson might well have been for naught. Nearctic's very existence was in jeopardy six months before he was born. His guardian angel was that gentle and unassuming horseman Harry Green, the stallion manager of the National Stud.

In the summer of 1953, Harry was dispatched to Montreal to collect several horses arriving from England. The first horse off the ship was a gift to Taylor from Lord Derby, which Harry readily loaded into his horse van. He then returned to the pier and sat down on an old wooden crate to wait for his other two passengers, a mare and foal. After some time, as Harry was becoming concerned, one of the ship's crew rushed down the gangplank and asked Harry if he would come aboard to speak with the first mate. It seems they were having difficulty with one of the animals.

Harry joined the first mate at the rim of the hatch overlooking the ship's vast hold. 'Even from where I was standing,' recounted Harry, 'three storeys up, I could see that the mare was in a lather. She was frantic, slipping and sliding all over the steel floor.'

Harry shouted down to the crew to put her back in her stall and quickly ran down the narrow metal stairs. The mare was shaking in fear and rage, her eyes were wild, and sweat was streaming off her body. The deckhands had been trying to force her into the shipping crate that would convey her up and out of the ship.

Harry didn't know anything about unloading ships, but he knew as much as anyone on the planet about transporting horses. This mare, like any other, would not go anywhere without her foal. Harry went into the stall to settle the half-crazed animal. When she calmed down and began to breathe normally he walked the foal into the crate.

'I was worried that the netting the crew were putting over the crate might frighten the little fellow,' Harry continued, 'so I asked the first mate for permission to ride up in the crate with the foal. He didn't like the idea, but he finally agreed, as long as I realised they couldn't be responsible if something happened to me.'

The foal was frightened and nickered to its mother. Nor was Harry too pleased at being hoisted up and out of the cargo area, swung over the deck, and lowered to the dock. But he focused on keeping the foal calm. Once Harry had the foal secured in the horse van he hurried back for the mare. This time, anxious to get to her foal, she walked willingly into the crate, with Harry by her side, patting and reassuring her, until they, too, were lowered safely to the dock.

The mare was Lady Angela; the foal was Empire Day. And in Lady Angela's belly was Nearctic. Lady Angela was five months pregnant. She had endured the trauma of a transatlantic crossing and a frenzied battle to stay with her foal. She might easily have miscarried or been seriously hurt but for Harry Green.

Harry looked after Nearctic for the eight years between the time the horse was retired to stud and his syndication for $1 million in 1968, when he was sent to stand at Mrs Richard C. du Pont's Woodstock Farm in Maryland. When Harry retired, he and his wife, Florence, drove to Maryland to visit his old friend Nearctic. It had been six years since Harry had seen the now ageing stallion. As he and Florence approached the barn, one of Mrs du Pont's staff rushed across the yard and politely suggested that the strangers return during visiting hours.

Harry explained they had driven a long way to see Nearctic. Harry was too modest to mention he had looked after Nearctic in Canada. Suddenly there was a loud nickering from the barn. After all those years, Nearctic had recognised Harry's voice. Harry once again asked if they could see Nearctic, and the groom agreed. As Harry entered the barn Nearctic struggled to his feet, bellowing and snorting. Harry finally confessed that he had once cared for Nearctic and asked if he might go into Nearctic's stall. Reluctantly the groom assented, adding, 'At your own risk, sir.' Although twenty and ailing, Nearctic was still volatile.

'Hello, Nicky, it's good to see you,' said Harry, opening the stall door and walking slowly toward the stallion. Nostrils flaring with excitement, eyes bright, Nearctic hobbled up to Harry and butted him with his snout. Harry responded by stroking him on the neck. Soon Nearctic was nuzzling at Harry's pockets to see if his old friend had brought him any treats. He had. It wasn't long before Nearctic allowed Harry to wrap his arms around the stallion's neck. Tears streamed down Harry's cheeks. He truly loved the horse. And in his way Nearctic loved Harry. Did the old horse know somehow that had it not been for Harry, he might never have been born?

Lady Angela gave birth to Nearctic on 11 February 1954, at the National Stud Farm. He grew to over sixteen hands high, with a brown coat so dark it was almost black. His handsome head, typical of Nearco's offspring, was long and narrow. He had a small V-shaped white marking in the centre of his forehead and a snip of white at the tip of his muzzle. Short white socks capped his hind legs from the top of the hoof over the fetlocks.

Windfields and the National Stud were producing far more horses than Taylor could possibly race in the turquoise-and-gold Windfields colours, so each fall he offered all his yearlings for sale at set prices. He valued Nearctic at $35,000. A few considered buying him, but none did: so Nearctic was sent to Pete McCann to train with the rest of the Windfields racers.

Like his sire, Nearco, Nearctic was tough. McCann claimed Nearctic had a 'mean streak', like most really good horses he had known, which compelled him to finish ahead of the others. His aggressiveness didn't stop with other horses: he didn't take kindly to humans pushing and pulling and telling him what to do; nor did the conventional North American-style of training at the track agree with his disposition.

Thoroughbreds in Europe are ridden out in the early morning and exercised over the gallops at home or designated training areas, such as Britain's gently rolling Newmarket Heath. In North America most conditioning is done right at the racetrack, the training ground generally limited to the oval track. Starting at daybreak at Woodbine, for example, a steady stream of thoroughbreds walk, jog, or buck and plunge along the roadways and on to the training track. The energy is palpable, and the excitement can put highly strung and volatile horses like Nearctic right over the top.

Nearctic fought his jockeys and exercise riders almost every stride of the way. He resisted the bit by running with his head upstretched. If his rider tried to get him under control by taking a stronger hold on the reins, the ever anxious Nearctic countered by leaping and climbing wildly through the air. Although some trainers saddle up their own placid stable ponies to accompany their horses for the morning workout, most prefer to keep their feet on the ground. Pete McCann, however, rode his charges himself, as often as he could. He was still training and riding wild-eyed two-year-olds before dawn at Woodbine when he was in his eighties.

Pete rode and worked with Nearctic almost daily, and much of the colt's early success must be attributed to Pete's dedication and ability to stick to the saddle of this often wild speedster. When Nearctic went to Saratoga to prepare for several big races, Taylor stabled him with US trainer Charley Shaw. Nearctic won the Saratoga Special, finished fourth in the Hopeful Stakes, and returned to Canada more crazed than ever. Back with McCann, he won the Carleton Stakes before showing signs of a quarter crack in his left front hoof, a stress-related injury that seven years later would also sideline Northern Dancer. (Technical advances in treating quarter cracks would allow Northern Dancer to resume racing, but in Nearctic's day, time was the only healer.)

At the end of his two-year-old season Nearctic had won seven races, four of them stakes races, and was declared Canadian champion. He was the first of Lady Angela's foals to become a racehorse, vindicating Taylor's determination to breed her to Nearco one more time, and was on his way to becoming the first successful result of breeding Nearco to a mare sired by Hyperion.

While Nearctic was back on the farm convalescing, Horatio Luro, the dapper Argentine trainer, arrived at Woodbine to run Eugenia II in the Canadian Championship, the forerunner of the Grade I Rothmans International Stakes. Eugenia II won the race and, at the victory party hosted by the Ontario Jockey Club, Taylor met and congratulated Luro.

Several weeks later the two met again, quite by accident, in a doctor's office in New York City. Eventually the conversation came around to Nearctic. Taylor had high hopes, but was concerned about the headstrong colt. During the winter Luro trained his horses in California and offered to take Nearctic with him.

'At that time, we thought we had ourselves a Kentucky Derby colt in Nearctic,' said Joe Thomas, Taylor's racing manager, 'and we let

Horatio take him . . . Certainly we felt he was a Queen's Plate winner.'

Luro had watched Nearctic in the mornings at Saratoga and felt the sharp and fast workouts he was receiving were what was making him overeager and out of control. Putting a racing edge on Nearctic was both foolish and dangerous. What Nearctic needed were long, slow gallops. But not one of Luro's exercise riders – nor anyone else he knew – was up to the task. Nearctic had become almost impossible to ride.

Luro was pondering this dilemma on the back stretch at Santa Anita, when his prayers were answered in the person of champion European jockey Rae Johnstone. Australian-born, 'Le Crocodile', as he was called by French racing fans, had ridden to some thirty classic victories. He frequently spent his winters in California and occasionally drove out to Santa Anita to exercise a horse or two to keep himself fit. Luro was convinced that Le Crocodile was the man for Nearctic, and the champion jockey accepted the challenge.

Every morning at eight sharp Luro tossed him up on to Nearctic's saddle and off they went. Instead of riding jockey-style, stirrups short, and crouched over the colt's withers, Johnstone rode with a loose rein and long stirrups, like a person out for a leisurely trot in the country. Johnstone sat on the nervous colt with ease and confidence, and kept him far away from anything that might upset him. For at least an hour the pair hacked aimlessly about the hilly wooded area around the track and over the turf course, sometimes walking, sometimes jogging. Other times Johnstone allowed Nearctic to stand still and listen to the early-morning sounds. When he felt Nearctic was relaxed and ready, he rode him over to the main track. Nearctic galloped around the track, easy and controlled.

Horatio Luro reported to Taylor that Nearctic had settled down, and was training extremely well. Now that confidence in Nearctic had been restored it was hoped that he would become a Kentucky Derby contender. The dream died that spring, shortly after Rae Johnstone returned to France for the beginning of the racing season. With Johnstone's patience and understanding, Nearctic had calmed down completely, so Luro put Nearctic back in training with the rest of the horses. It wasn't long before the quarter crack resurfaced: Nearctic was lame. The Kentucky Derby was now out of the question.

He did race that year, however, and not surprisingly won only four of his thirteen starts. One of his victories was in the mile-and-one-sixteenth International Handicap, which he took by an amazing six lengths, equalling the Canadian record. In another race at Woodbine he set a new track record for six and a half furlongs.

It wasn't until Nearctic's fourth year that he started to mature into a powerful and confident champion. That season he won his first five starts with authority; then he faltered, perhaps because too much was being asked of him. His first defeat was the Dominion Day Handicap at Woodbine on 1 July. He finished fourth, a length and a quarter behind the winner. Four days later he was back for the Connaught Cup. He came in sixth.

His next race was the Michigan Mile, 18 July at Detroit. Nearctic broke in front, stayed there, and scorched across the finish lengths ahead of a field that included Mister Jive, Swoon's Son and Red God. With his victory also came the then richest purse won by a Canadian horse, $40,000.

In the spring of the following year, Nearctic won the Vigil Handicap at Woodbine, a six-furlong sprint, and equalled the track record while carrying top weight of 126 pounds. In his next race he was third, and in his final race, the Ultimus Handicap, Nearctic finished sixth, and lame. His racing days were over. His limbs were no longer able to keep up with his will to win. He had started 47 times, won 21 races, was placed 5 times, and was third 3 times.

Nearctic was retired to the National Stud Farm, and began his new role as stallion in the spring of 1960. His first crop of foals yielded four stakes winners: Langcrest, Pierlou, Arctic Hills and Northern Dancer. Nearctic's prominence in thoroughbred history has from the outset been obscured by his most famous son. Yet at the 1992 July yearlings sales at Keeneland, more than two-thirds of the élite young thoroughbreds on offer had Nearctic in their pedigree through sons Northern Dancer, Icecapade and Explodent.

None of this would have happened, however, had Nearctic not won the Michigan Mile, and thus provided the dowry that brought the dam of Northern Dancer to Windfields.

During the first week of August 1958, two weeks after Nearctic won the Michigan Mile, Taylor was at the yearling sales at Saratoga, New York. He had decided to invest Nearctic's $40,000 winnings and he was determined to buy something special.

He didn't need another horse as the stalls at Windfields were full;

however, since he was committed to raising a classic winner in Canada, he focused on building a first-class herd of brood mares. In fact, he bought only fillies. Saratoga was an annual excursion. He and Mrs Taylor drove to this famed spa area each summer for the sales, the races, and the festivities.

The special yearling he finally settled on was a bay filly with one white stocking, a large star on her forehead, and a white snip on her face that grew larger as it wrapped down and around her muzzle. She cost $35,000, and they named her Natalma. The female side of her pedigree was powerful. She was the third foal of Almahmoud, the stakes winning daughter of English Derby winner Mahmoud. Almahmoud's first foal was stakes winner Cosmah, dam of two-time champion Tosmah, and Halo, sire of champions, including Sunny Silence, Sunny's Halo, Glorious Song and Devil's Bag.

Natalma was also a granddaughter of Mother Goose, who astounded the fans at Belmont in 1924 when she screeched first across the wire in the Futurity, a 29-horse cavalry charge of North America's top colts and fillies. Mother Goose is recognised as one of the continent's most important taproot mares, from whom generations of outstanding thoroughbreds are traced.

Natalma's sire, Native Dancer, was the most exciting and brilliant horse to gallop North America's oval tracks since Man O' War. The strapping 16.3-hand steel-grey colt thundered on to the scene just as television began to cover major North American horse races. Native Dancer was an instant television idol.

Foaled in 1950 in Maryland at Alfred G. Vanderbilt's Sagamore Farm, Native Dancer was incomparable as a two-year-old. Confident and calm, he romped to victory in all nine starts, barely working up a sweat despite carrying as much as 130 pounds. The other North American two-year-olds became accustomed to following his flowing grey tail across the finish.

At three he emerged bigger, stronger, more heavily muscled and built to run easily over any distance. He won the Belmont, the Preakness, the Wood Memorial – every one of the twenty-two races he entered, except one. The Kentucky Derby of '53 is still considered the greatest upset in the history of the race. A literal 'dark horse' named Dark Star stole across the finish inches ahead of Native Dancer. Legend has it that the 'Grey Ghost of Sagamore' still lurks beneath the ancient stands of Churchill Downs, seeking revenge.

Native Dancer was reputed to disdain humans. He made a game of picking up hapless grooms in his teeth and flinging them through the air like rag dolls. He hated the whip: he wasn't about to take orders from the pint-sized mortals on his back. Exercise riders were ever vigilant lest they become victims in another of his games: he would swing his mighty head around, clamp his jaws around a boot, haul the rider out of the saddle, and drop him or her indelicately on the ground. When Native Dancer was in his paddock, he strolled over to the gate to be led into the barn at feeding time only when he was good and ready.

He seems to have had far greater tolerance for kittens than humans. The first time a litter of barn kittens clambered into his stall, the staff thought he might kill them. Instead he appeared to enjoy their company, and his stall became their regular playground.

Native Dancer was a warrior, an animal vastly superior to every other racehorse of his generation. As a stallion, he continued his supremacy: sons of the 'Grey Ghost of Sagamore', Kauai King (1966) and Dancer's Image (1968), won the Kentucky Derby (although Dancer's Image was later disqualified); as did grandsons Northern Dancer (1964) and Majestic Prince (1969); and great-grand-daughter Genuine Risk (1980), great-grandsons Affirmed (1978) and Alysheba (1987). Ferdinand (1986) and Sea Hero (1993) are also descendants of Native Dancer.

He was the sire of European classic winner Hula Dancer and grandsire of Epsom Derby winner Sea Bird II. His daughter Shenanigans was the dam of Ruffian, while Natalma was the dam of Northern Dancer.

Natalma was vanned from the Saratoga sales to Windfields to spend the autumn and winter with the other yearling fillies. As Natalma matured, E.P. Taylor felt she had such promise that rather than start her racing career in Canada, as was his custom with his horses, he sent her to Horatio Luro to be trained and raced in the United States.

In the spring of 1959, Natalma won her first two starts in New York at Belmont; with Bobby Ussery in the irons, she took the Spinaway Stakes at Saratoga by three-quarters of a length. The horses had no sooner jogged back in front of the crowd to be unsaddled than the track announcer declared there was an 'inquiry'. Coming out of the back stretch, Ussery had cracked Natalma with his whip. In an effort to avoid it, Natalma had ducked to the inside, bumping the filly Warlike and causing her to hit the inside rail. Natalma was disqualified for interference.

Soon after the race Luro sailed to France to escape his allergy to North American ragweed. His assistant, Thomas 'Peaches' Flemming, was left in charge. When Luro returned to Belmont several weeks later he discovered that Natalma had gone on strike. Every morning she was fed, watered and groomed. Every morning she was saddled and bridled. Every morning an exercise rider was tossed up into her saddle. And every morning Natalma refused to go near the track.

It seems that she equated racetracks with Ussery's whipping, and wanted nothing more to do with them. (In trying to get her to the track, the exercise riders might also have resorted to the whip, which would have compounded the problem.)

Luro knew that the only way he could coax Natalma near a track again was to win her trust and defuse her anxiety. So every morning he gave her a mild tranquilliser, got on his pony, and casually escorted Natalma and her rider on a tour of the Belmont stable area. At first they went nowhere near the track, strolled along the shed-row, where Luro stopped and chatted leisurely with other trainers. Natalma was allowed to graze or stand idly watching and listening to the early-morning activities. Eventually, Luro and his pony escorted Natalma and her rider out to the track at the end of each stroll. As her stress decreased, Natalma gradually consented to resume training, and as her confidence returned, the social calls were phased out.

All was going well until the morning Natalma pulled up lame. The diagnosis: a small bone chip in her right knee. Natalma was sent to the veterinary clinic at the University of Pennsylvania to have the chip removed. The operation was a success and Natalma was returned to Canada to recuperate.

In the spring of 1960, Natalma was shipped back to Luro at Kentucky's Keeneland track to train for the Kentucky Oaks. Her travelling companion was a powerful bay colt called Victoria Park. An exceptional racehorse, and a prophet of things to come, the Canadian-bred Victoria Park was being prepped for the Kentucky Derby.

Natalma's long convalescence and the relaxed Keeneland training atmosphere had her in shape and ready for the Kentucky Oaks. In fact, Natalma and Victoria Park were looking so good that Luro began to dream of winning the 'Kentucky Double': the Oaks and the Derby.

Six days prior to her big race, Luro worked Natalma a mile on the Churchill Downs track. The stop-watches clicked at 1.37. Natalma was quick, fit – and lame. A calcium deposit had formed on the knee that had undergone surgery.

With the first half of Luro's Kentucky Double sidelined, all efforts focused on Victoria Park. He was third in the Kentucky Derby, a fast-closing second in the Preakness, and favoured to win the Belmont. Although convinced Victoria Park would take the Belmont, Taylor brought his colt home to Canada. The Queen's Plate was scheduled on the same day as the Belmont, and the Queen Mother was to be guest of honour.

Bringing back Victoria Park proved a controversial decision, and an avalanche of mail arrived at Windfields, some condemning, some praising. One letter was addressed to 'Mr. E.P. Taylor, Horseman (1st) and Beer Baron (2nd), Toronto, Canada'. Scrawled across the envelope was the message 'Postmaster – I do not know the address. Please look it up and put two bucks on his horse.' Also in the mail was a death threat against Victoria Park's jockey, Avelino Gomez.

Potential assassins would have had to be crack shots on Queen's Plate day. Victoria Park left the rest of the field coughing up his dust as he set a new track record and lightened the Buckingham Palace bank account by fifty guineas, the annual royal gift to the winner.

Natalma accompanied Victoria Park throughout his US Triple Crown challenge. She trained at Keeneland with him, was stabled in the next stall at Churchill Downs, travelled to Baltimore with him for the Preakness, and came back to Canada with him before the Queen's Plate. The horse van dropped Victoria Park off at Woodbine Racetrack and continued down the highway to Oshawa: Natalma arrived at the National Stud Farm on 15 June 1960.

Several days earlier, Taylor had met with his key personnel at the old stone house on the farm. The lengthy agenda included Natalma's future, and the consensus was that her brief racing career was over: she would be retired to the brood mare band. The Windfields team was then faced with a decision: should they breed her now or wait until next year?

The middle of June is late in the season to breed thoroughbred racehorses, since on 1 January all thoroughbreds in the northern hemisphere are designated a year older. Thus a foal born in January and one born the following May are officially the same age. In the early stages of a horse's development, such an age gap can be significant. In the wild, horses breed mainly in May and June. Given the 11-month gestation horses have, breeding at that time of the year ensures that foals will be born when there is a good supply of fresh, nutritious spring grass.

There were other variables to consider as well: first, Natalma would have to come into heat; second, she would have to be impregnated on her first breeding. Therefore the services of an extremely potent stallion were required. Luckily they had the perfect candidate: in this, his first year at stud, Nearctic had already proven himself supremely virile.

PART TWO
Northern Dancer: Larger Than Life

A horse runs with its lungs,
perseveres with its heart,
and wins with its character.

Federico Tesio

Every once in a long, long time, something special happens that through its very nature alters our perceptions forever. In this case it was a little horse, Northern Dancer, that not only transformed an entire sport, but challenged our preconceptions, our ability to see beyond the obvious.

Northern Dancer certainly proved he could run a hole through the wind, but perhaps what made this animal more remarkable was that he was disadvantaged, at least in the eyes of many of his beholders. He simply didn't look like an elegant, majestic thoroughbred. Like Hyperion, Selene, and other great but small horses, he was derogated as a potential racehorse, much less a champion, over and over. And by the time it became apparent that Northern Dancer was a great racehorse, his racing days had come to an end.

The Little Horse No One Wanted

27 MAY 1961
NATIONAL STUD FARM, OSHAWA, ONTARIO

The tiny newborn lay in a thick bed of fresh straw, close to his mother. Exhausted from giving birth to her first foal, Natalma was stretched out on her side. Her dark brown hide was soaking wet from the exertion and her large belly heaved as she tried to catch her breath, yet within seconds she was calling her foal with short, throaty nickers. It was 12.15 a.m., and assistant farm manager Peter Poole was in the stall with Natalma and her little foal.

During his rounds earlier in the evening, Peter had noticed Natalma was becoming anxious, restless – it was only a matter of time. He would monitor the mare throughout the long night ahead.

Three out of four thoroughbred mares give birth between 11 p.m. and 2.30 a.m. Scientists contend that the foetus, through its hormones acting on the mare's uterus, determines the time of birth, but most people who work with horses believe the mare decides. Her inner guidance system, they believe, knows it is safest to give birth at night, when the threat of predators is least.

As horses are flight animals, the only real defence against danger they have is to run. Giving birth at night ensures that by morning – when predators are most active – the foal will be up on its feet and able to run with its mother.

By 11.30 p.m. Natalma had become agitated. She was sweating, and kicking at her large belly; she had never experienced the cramping and other physical sensations that are part of giving birth. Earlier, milk had dripped from her swollen udder; now it poured out, as Natalma circled the large stall. Soon she experienced her first contraction. The second one came about five minutes later. After another five minutes the mare's waters broke.

A foal lives upside-down in the womb, but turns just before labour begins to an upright position, with its head and forelegs extended. Within moments a tiny hoof appeared, still encased in the amniotic sac. Then it retracted. Natalma kept circling the stall looking for the right place to lie down. The foal's small hoof continued to appear and disappear as the contractions became more frequent. Natalma finally collapsed and rolled over on her side with a groan. The real work was about to begin.

The first tiny hoof was followed by a second. Then the muzzle appeared and slowly the foal's entire head slid into view, nostrils twitching and sniffing. It opened its eyes and blinked its long eyelashes repeatedly in an attempt to adjust to the lights in the barn. Natalma gave a great push: now the foal's front legs, neck and shoulders were out. She rested for a few minutes, gave one mighty heave, and the foal was lying on the ground. It was a tiny bay colt with three white socks. A narrow blaze, which began beneath his curly black forelock, ran down his face and across his left nostril. The angle of the marking gave him a cheeky, impudent look.

Peter Poole immediately clamped the umbilical cord and disinfected the foal's navel with ferric chloride. The little colt's thick coat was curly and wet. Peter dried him off with a large terry-cloth towel. Finally he gave the colt tetanus and penicillin shots in its hip.

It took Natalma about ten minutes to regain her strength before she climbed back on to her feet to nuzzle and gently lick her foal. Her urging nickers, and his own instincts, told the little colt that he had to get on his feet immediately.

Foals are born with legs two-thirds their adult length so that in case of danger they can cover the same amount of ground at the gallop as their mothers. Their long legs make sense for survival, but trying to stand up on them for the first time must be like learning to get up on stilts. The foal has to hoist a small peanut-shaped body up on four long, spindly legs that tend to slide in all directions at once. The process can take hours. Not so with Natalma's son.

On his first attempt, the colt pushed his two front legs out in front of him. Then he hauled himself up so he was sitting on his haunches, looking like a bewildered puppy. He gathered his strength and determination, and attempted to hoist his back end up to the level of his front end. He got halfway there, and splat, down he went, landing face first in the bed of straw. He blinked, snorted, shook his head, and started again. And again. With one final burst of energy he was up, wobbling around on his four stilts: it had taken him less than ten minutes. He then let out his first triumphant whinny.

Now his instincts compelled him to seek out nutrition. He teetered over to Natalma and began to explore. His little nose twitched and sniffed – at her shoulders, her legs, her hips, her flanks, even her tail. Every time he got close to her tender udder, Natalma flinched. The colt persevered and, with some help from Peter Poole, connected with the food supply.

Two days later Natalma and her foal were turned out in the paddock next to the foaling barn. Later that week, Natalma and her energetic youngster were led down the lane to join a small band of mares and colts grazing over a large pasture.

In the beginning, the colt seldom strayed far from Natalma's side. There is an invisible boundary – the 'mum zone', a circle around the mare – within which the foal feels safe. For the first few weeks the perimeter extends only a few feet from the mare. If a foal suddenly finds itself beyond the circumference it will come screeching back to the mum zone.

As the weeks go by the circle expands, and it isn't long before the foal, ever curious and energetic, begins cavorting with the other foals. When their energy is spent, they return to their mum zone, collapse on to the grass, and fall into a deep sleep, protected by their ever vigilant dams. Once recharged, they scramble back up on to their long legs, to resume their games.

That autumn Natalma's foal, and all the others, were weaned from their mothers. By then they had grown independent, and spent most of their time together, running and kicking up their tiny heels. And they had learned to eat grass – no easy feat given the length of their legs. It requires splaying the front legs precariously wide in order to stretch the short neck and head to the ground.

The weaning happened over a week. Each day one of the mares was taken from the herd and moved to a distant paddock, until the foals were completely on their own. Natalma's colt and the other young males would spend the winter together: housed in the same barn at night, grazing the same pasture by day, sparring, like young fighters preparing for a title match. The innately wild nature of male horses causes them to 'train' for the day they will challenge the established stallion for all or part of the herd.

It's not certain who gave Natalma's colt the name Northern Dancer, but it was likely Winifred Taylor. She had come up with the name Windfields for the farm, and in later years, each autumn, she could be found in the den by the coffee table cluttered with papers and books, trying to find names for the latest group of Windfields runners. She made a game of the naming, and invited anyone interested to join in the fun. Then she submitted three names, in order of preference, for each horse, to the Jockey Club for approval. Thus the bay colt, out of Natalma by Nearctic, was given the name Northern Dancer.

It's hard to imagine a more fitting name for this cheeky little Canadian colt, for he would spend winter days cavorting with the other colts in the deep snow that blanketed the Windfields paddocks, and would learn to keep his balance when ice storms transformed pathways into skating rinks, and the spring thaw turned patches of the paddocks into mud slicks. Several months prior to the annual sale of yearlings, and before they inflicted too many cuts and scrapes on one another, Northern Dancer and the rest of the colts were separated into individual paddocks.

'Northern Dancer was a real devil,' recalled yearling manager André Blaettler, 'especially when it came time to come into the barn. He'd be flying around the paddock with that choppy gait of his – I thought he looked like a hackney pony – and then he'd come skidding to a halt at the gate. He'd rear. No one wanted to bring him in on their own.'

André Blaettler was possibly one of the first to be deceived by Northern Dancer's looks, but he would eventually be joined by a large crowd. A group of Canadian thoroughbred experts were about to distinguish themselves as the ones who turned their backs on the greatest horse deal in history.

16 SEPTEMBER 1962
WINDFIELDS FARM, TORONTO, ONTARIO

Northern Dancer stood at the far end of the black tarmac path. Gathered along either side of the runway were several hundred people, some sitting in rows of red-and-white striped canvas chairs, others milling behind. The occasion was the ninth annual sale of Windfields yearlings. One of the three top-priced animals in the sale, he was obviously one of Taylor's favourites. Yet no one understood why he was valued so highly. He certainly didn't look the part.

Northern Dancer appeared anxious. Like all skittish thoroughbreds, he could be thrown into a frenzy by anything out of the norm, even an unfamiliar piece of paper at the side of a familiar path. Today, the peaceful environment he was accustomed to buzzed with the excitement and anticipation of the buyers and spectators who had converged on the farm for the event.

While Northern Dancer waited his turn to parade before the potential buyers, his groom patted his neck and tried to calm the colt. His bay hide had been curried again and again; now, in the late-afternoon sun, it shone like copper. His neatly trimmed black mane lay flat against his already powerful young neck. He wore a brand-new leather head collar, and a breaking bit.

The sale was being conducted on the lawns and garden area between the rectangular red-brick stables. Each of the many green-shingled steeples bore a weather vane with a horse motif. Beyond the barns, white board fences cordoned off the paddocks where Northern Dancer and the rest of the yearlings had spent the past year.

E.P. Taylor stood at the head of the walkway, a red carnation in his tweed jacket lapel. Taylor was 63 now, and quite portly. Beside him was his tall, lean racing manager, Joe Thomas, who with Taylor had assigned a price to each of the horses. They had valued Northern Dancer at $25,000.

As the groom led Northern Dancer down the path between the buyers and spectators, Thomas, a former Kentucky newspaperman, told the audience about the colt's lineage. Northern Dancer, like the other yearlings, had a round number tag dangling from his halter that corresponded to his listing in the catalogue so potential buyers could readily identify him.

He was, however, easily recognisable. Northern Dancer didn't look like any of the other yearlings. He was obviously the shortest, standing fourteen hands, two and a half inches high (about four feet ten inches). He weighed 955 pounds, about 40 pounds less than average, and looked far more like a 'quarter horse' than a thoroughbred.

A bundle of anxious and explosive energy, Northern Dancer pranced down the runway; then his groom returned him to the stables, where a parade of prospective buyers (and the merely inquisitive) strolled up and down the wide aisles.

Divining a champion from a herd of young thoroughbreds is

logically impossible. There are the obvious criteria, such as bloodlines and conformation but, in the end, it's not what's in the catalogue or visible to the naked eye that counts, but what's inside the animal: the will to win.

Buying a yearling is always a gamble, if at times a rewarding one. In 1954, the first year of the sale, Bill Beasley, whose amusement empire included carousels and bingo parlours at Toronto's Canadian National Exhibition, gambled a mere $7,500 on a bay colt. Canadian Champ captured the Canadian Triple Crown (Queen's Plate Stakes, Prince of Wales Stakes, Breeders' Stakes). He won $150,000 for Beasley, and earned another $60,000 when Taylor bought the horse back to stand at stud.

Beasley's good fortune and the fact that animals born and bred at Windfields were by far the best racehorses in Canada were reasons enough to lure buyers in increasing numbers each year. But perhaps there was an even more seductive element: 'the one that got away'.

In the six years since Canadian Champ had won the Queen's Plate, four other winners of Canadian racing's most prestigious prize had been offered at the Windfields sale: Lyford Cay (1957), New Providence (1959), Victoria Park (1960), and Flaming Page (1962). All except Flaming Page were, for one reason or another, overlooked or dismissed by the buyers. Frank Sherman bought Flaming Page but returned her because she had a mildly inflamed fetlock. Taylor graciously replaced her with another filly of Sherman's choice. Flaming Page not only won the Queen's Plate, but was voted Horse of the Year and, when she stopped kicking Northern Dancer in the ribs and the two finally mated, produced Nijinsky, the first British Triple Crown winner in 35 years.

Like prospectors looking for gold, the buyers at Windfields stopped at every stall, peering in, consulting their catalogues, their trainers, their instincts. When they came upon a yearling they were interested in, a groom would take the animal outside and walk it up and down the path by the barn. When they arrived at Northern Dancer's stall, they saw that his pedigree was impressive, but both his parents had been erratic or disappointing: Nearctic because of his quarter crack and training difficulties, Natalma because of her knee injury. Jim Boylen remembers the sale well: he was one of those scrutinising both the colt and the catalogue.

'I was at the sale with my brother Phil and our trainer, Art

Warner. We actually considered buying Northern Dancer. We liked his breeding, but our trainer advised us against it. "Who wants a midget?" he said.

'All I can say is it's a good thing we didn't buy him. We were just a bunch of amateurs. Knowing us we probably would have gelded him.'

Larkin Maloney seriously considered buying the colt, but he, too, was talked out of it by his trainer. Instead his trainer recommended he spend his $25,000 on another of the top-priced horses in the sale, a lanky son of Menetrier. Maloney called him Brockton Boy, and there's no telling what he must have thought as he watched Northern Dancer fly past his colt – or past the Kentucky Derby finishing post.

Taylor had devised the sales format because his breeding programme, designed to create a Kentucky Derby winner in Canada, was producing far more horses than his stable could accommodate. Yet he knew that the friends and racing associates he invited to buy his yearlings would be sceptical unless he offered every one of them for sale. The risk, of course, was breeding a Kentucky Derby winner that would run in someone else's colours. That year, 14 buyers purchased a total of 15 yearlings. The remaining 33 would train and race for Windfields Farm. Among them was Northern Dancer.

Two weeks later the unsold yearlings were loaded on to the horse van for delivery to the Windfields training division across York Mills Road, a major thoroughfare that ran through the rambling Windfields property. Their days of cavorting and grazing freely in Windfields' lush paddocks were over. During the next few weeks they would slowly be introduced to bridles, saddles and, finally, riders.

Northern Dancer was barely 16 months old, but half a ton of solid muscle and willpower. Joe Thomas described the colt as a 'wilful son of a gun'. He claimed, 'He wasn't mean or anything, but he'd do tricks.' The exercise riders were far less flattering. Each morning three separate sets of ten to twelve yearlings went in a group to work in the indoor riding enclosure. When the horses were being assigned Northern Dancer was always chosen last: no one wanted to ride him, and with good cause.

The first time Northern Dancer was ridden, the exercise boy took a short hold on the reins and gave the colt a couple of nudges with his heels to urge him forward. And forward they went. The volatile colt exploded. He lunged straight up, plunged, then bucked, catapulting the rider through the air before the poor fellow came crashing to the ground. Once rid of the bothersome human, Northern Dancer careered around the riding arena, galloping and bucking, the stirrups flapping against the saddle and the reins dangling dangerously beneath his outstretched muzzle. As he sailed past the other yearlings, they, too, began to buck and spin. Finally someone was able to grab his dangling reins and pull him up. Peace was restored temporarily.

Sitting on Northern Dancer's back was akin to straddling a powder keg. When he trotted he didn't glide forward, he bounced from one hoof to the next. When he broke into a canter, he'd go a couple of strides, then *boom*, he'd explode. Powerful and agile, he could stop, turn on a dime or fly off in the opposite direction. He wanted little to do with training, and did not endear himself to his handlers.

Yet in the end, all these characteristics, both physical and mental, were what made him extraordinary.

'Our Last Hope'

Diary of the Two-Year-Old Season

21 MARCH 1963
WOODBINE RACETRACK, TORONTO

Around mid-morning Northern Dancer arrived at Woodbine, about a half-hour's drive from Windfields along Highway 401 in Toronto. For young horses the back stretch of most North American tracks is an environmental shock, like moving from the country to the city; the pastoral serenity of the farm is replaced with a new energy. At Woodbine not only are there 1,500 horses stabled, there are also the thousands of men and women who serve the horses. Each trainer has a team of grooms, hot-walkers, exercise riders; veterinarians and blacksmiths constantly make their rounds; jockeys' agents negotiate mounts for their riders; forklifts haul bins of straw and manure away to mushroom growers; trucks carry orders of hay, straw and grain; the carrot man comes by with his bushel baskets; a few blasts on the snack-truck horn draws workers from their chores for coffee in a paper cup timed to collapse on the last sip. A steady flow of announcements crackles over the public-address system from the racing secretary's office.

Activity starts long before daybreak. In March it may begin with the grooms chipping through the ice that has formed overnight on the water buckets. The mornings are dark, cold and damp. There's mud everywhere.

Yet for racetrackers it's an optimistic time: a new season. And with it comes the dream that one of the horses they are training, riding or grooming will be a stakes winner, perhaps even a champion. In the warmth of the track kitchen fried eggs and bacon sizzle on the griddle, bitter black coffee steams in giant urns, and small groups gather at the Arborite tables where often the conversation will turn to their hopes for the coming season.

Because 1 January is the official birthday for all thoroughbreds born in the northern hemisphere, Northern Dancer was now in his two-year-old year of racing. He was one of several young Windfields horses rejected at the 1962 sale to be trained by Horatio Luro. ('It seemed logical to send him to Luro,' explained racing manager Joe Thomas, 'as he'd trained the dam and had had such bad luck with her.')

The remainder of the Windfields herd were under the care of resident trainer Pete McCann. Luro stayed in California with his other owners' horses, and his assistant, Peaches Flemming, was sent to look after the horses in Canada.

Each morning at Woodbine, once the horses are watered, fed and groomed, they are saddled, bridled and ridden out to train, individually or in small groups. There are horses everywhere: some galloping around the oval track; others on the way to the training track; the rest returning. Young horses are frequently overwhelmed by their new surroundings and respond by bucking and shying, often with little obvious provocation.

When they arrive back at the stables, their stalls have been mucked out. They will be groomed again, and bathed if it's warm enough. Before being put in their stalls, they will be walked around and around the shed-row, or stable area, to cool down.

Northern Dancer's training was, however, impeded by a recurring cracked heel, a form of psoriasis in the hollow at the back of the pastern (the short bone just above the hoof). The condition most frequently occurs in wet, cold weather and causes the skin to become reddened, scaly and tender. Blisters then form and, when they rupture, a crack appears. Once the infection sets in, it is easily irritated by dirt or sand and causes the horse to go lame.

It was months before Flemming felt that Northern Dancer could be safely worked without threat of further irritation.

8 JUNE 1963
WOODBINE RACETRACK

Northern Dancer ran his first official 'breeze': a workout during which the rider controls the horse's speed. On average, thoroughbreds can run a furlong (an eighth of a mile) in 12 seconds; most can run two furlongs in 24 seconds, but only top-calibre horses are able to maintain that speed over the longer distances. In North America these workouts serve to condition a horse for a race. The workouts are timed and published at the track and in the *Daily Racing Form* and become part of the horse's official record.

Northern Dancer galloped three furlongs over Woodbine's training track in 39.8 seconds, a respectable time, considering the track was slow and he was just beginning to train.

6 JULY 1963
WOODBINE RACETRACK

Northern Dancer's trademark explosive start out of the gate was first witnessed on this sunny July morning, barely a month after his first breeze.

He and two stable-mates jogged down the dirt road between the stables toward the main track, accompanied by Horatio Luro aboard a lead pony. Standard attire for most trainers riding out with their racehorses is a pair of leather chaps, cowboy boots and a helmet or baseball cap, but Luro looked straight out of *GQ*: shirt and tie, shiny tall riding boots, breeches, hacking jacket and tweed cap.

Although Northern Dancer had been walked in, out and around the starting gate to familiarise him with the contraption, this was to be his first break from the gate. Before Northern Dancer was led in, Luro called over his rider, Ramón Hernandez, to give him instructions. According to Joe Hirsch's biography of Luro, *The Grand Señor*, 'Luro said the colt was a little lazy and asked Hernandez to touch him on the shoulder with his whip at the start'.

Northern Dancer and his two stable-mates were secured in the starting gate, the loud bell clanged, and the stall doors sprang open. Immediately Hernandez slapped Northern Dancer on the shoulder with his whip.

When Hernandez finally caught his breath, he must have wondered where Luro had got the impression the colt was 'a little lazy'. Northern Dancer had taken off like a shot out of a cannon. He had, it seems, inherited Natalma's and Native Dancer's disdain for the whip.

With Hernandez standing in the stirrups, hauling on the reins with all his might, Northern Dancer simply set his jaw and kept going. There was no stopping him. He bolted three furlongs in 37 seconds – a couple of seconds off the track record.

13 JULY 1963
FORT ERIE RACETRACK, FORT ERIE, ONTARIO

Northern Dancer was shipped to Fort Erie to prepare for the summer race meet there, which would begin in early August.

A couple of weeks later, Northern Dancer's rider rode the colt up to the clocker's stand to report the horse's name and say that they were planning to breeze a half-mile out of the gate. The clocker is the track official responsible for timing the morning workouts of each horse. When the training track closes at 9 a.m. the clocker reports the information to the *Daily Racing Form* where it will appear in that day's edition of the paper.

The second the bell rang, Northern Dancer blasted out of the gate and the gentle breeze turned into a gale-force wind. Again he may have associated the starting bell with the whip, and before his rider knew what had happened, they were flying, out of control, past the other horses on the track. They sailed by the astonished clocker, who instinctively pressed the button at the top of his stop-watch. Northern Dancer's time was 48.8 seconds, one second off the track record; yet he had been in serious training less than two months. The horse's spectacular workout caught the attention of the *Daily Racing Form* editor that morning. It was of stakes calibre: this was a colt to watch.

The following morning, E.P. Taylor arrived at Fort Erie with the *Daily Racing Form* in his pocket. He toured the Windfields horses with racing manager Joe Thomas, who reported on the progress of the fifty-or-so Windfields horses in training. (Thomas also helped prepare the sales catalogues and any advertising or publicity material. Since Taylor was not disposed to be interviewed by the media, Thomas acted as spokesperson for Windfields.)

When they came to Northern Dancer's stall, Taylor wanted to know when they would enter the colt in his first race. Luro had gone to Europe, and had left instructions that Flemming was not to race the colt until he'd returned. He felt that Northern Dancer still needed time to mature: not only was he younger than other two-year-olds, but he had missed valuable conditioning time because of his cracked heel. But there was another reason to hold off: starting a horse as uncontrollable as Northern Dancer was dangerous both to the colt and to the other horses in the field.

According to Thomas, however, 'We thought we had some pretty good two-year-olds that year, but as the season wore on they fell by the wayside. Northern Dancer seemed pretty much our last hope.'

Flemming was still opposed to running Northern Dancer. He thought he was too unpredictable and inexperienced. Luro, now back from Europe and at Saratoga, agreed. Yet Thomas was anxious to see Northern Dancer up and racing, and stressed that they had to get going with him. 'Peaches [Flemming], of course, was pretty reluctant,' Thomas said. 'He told me that he thought he was still too green, but I said, "Oh, hell, go ahead and run him."'

2 AUGUST 1963
FORT ERIE RACETRACK

Early that afternoon Northern Dancer and the other two-year-olds scheduled for the third race were walked from the back stretch, on the far side of the track, around to the paddock by the grandstand, where the horses were to be saddled. The race was a five-and-a-half-furlong maiden (for horses that had not yet won a race) for horses foaled in Canada. A small crowd gathered around the paddock, and as Flemming tightened the wide overgirth (a second girth that is strapped over the tiny racing saddle for safety), Northern Dancer had his first experience of the highly charged energy created by fans prior to a race.

An official shouted, 'Riders up!' and Flemming tossed Northern Dancer's flyweight jockey up into the saddle. Wearing Windfields' turquoise-and-gold silks was a young apprentice from New Brunswick named Ron Turcotte, famous ten years later as the rider of Secretariat in his memorable US Triple Crown victories.

'The first time I rode Northern Dancer I knew he was something special,' recalled Turcotte. 'He broke sluggishly but lay third most of the way. When I called on him for extra, he moved to the lead immediately but was satisfied to stay head to head with the other horse. As I was instructed not to touch him with the whip, I refrained until we were past the 16th pole, then I decided to disregard orders and turned my stick up. In order not to be seen by the trainer or assistant trainer I quickly switched the stick to my left hand and tapped him one time.

'To my surprise he exploded, and within 70 yards he opened up an eight-length lead, which is what he won by. Had I done that at the quarter pole he surely would have won by 15 to 20 lengths!'

According to Joe Thomas in *Chronology of a Champion*, Northern Dancer had become, in one short race, Windfields' 'best two-year-old and its best prospect for the Summer Stakes'.

But being the 'best prospect' was a dubious distinction, given that the rest of Windfields' two-year-old crop had 'fallen by the wayside'. He was, in fact, merely their 'last hope'.

17 AUGUST 1963
FORT ERIE RACETRACK

The Summer Stakes was the biggest two-year-old purse offered at Fort Erie. Since Northern Dancer had raced only once, in preparation for the big event he was entered in the Vandal, a lesser stakes event with a considerably smaller prize. Ron Turcotte had a previous commitment, so Paul Bohenko was hired to ride the colt.

'I hated to miss Northern Dancer's next start,' recalled Turcotte, 'but I was under contract to ride for Addison Hall. Their horse, Ramblin' Road, had already broken a few track records. Northern Dancer got into a speed duel with Brockton Boy and they tired each other out so I came on the outside to win by three lengths.

'Even after defeating Northern Dancer with Ramblin' Road I told Mr Luro that the Dancer was definitely the best two-year-old in Canada, maybe in the world.'

Northern Dancer finished second in the Vandal Stakes, followed by Brockton Boy, the horse Larkin Maloney's trainer had advised him to buy instead of Northern Dancer.

24 AUGUST 1963
WOODBINE RACETRACK

Paul Bohenko was back in Northern Dancer's saddle for the Summer Stakes, a mile on the turf. Northern Dancer won, but the race took its toll. According to Thomas, 'The ground was bog deep . . . He kept almost falling down and picking himself up; yet he hung on to the lead all the way and won. We knew we had a pretty good horse.'

Luro, who had not yet seen the horse run, said, 'It was a spirited performance and Northern Dancer's people were encouraged, but it was also his third start in the month of August.' When Luro finally arrived, the first thing he ordered was 'a week or two of inactivity'.

28 SEPTEMBER 1963
WOODBINE RACETRACK

Ron Turcotte was back to ride Northern Dancer in the Cup and Saucer Stakes. A mile-and-one-sixteenth race over the turf, it is restricted to horses foaled in Canada and, with the Coronation Futurity, is one of the top races for two-year-olds. Because of his Summer Stakes win, the track handicappers loaded Northern Dancer down with top weight of 124 pounds. (Other horses were assigned as little as 113 pounds.)

Northern Dancer shot out of the gate and took the early lead, but as the pack thundered down to the wire he tired and was beaten by three-quarters of a length by Grand Garçon, a rank outsider that paid $91.50 on a $2.00 win ticket. By an obscure stallion named Censor, Grand Garçon was one of the 15 yearlings purchased at the 1962 Windfields sale. Frank Sherman paid $10,000 for the colt that had beaten Northern Dancer.

7 OCTOBER 1963
WOODBINE RACETRACK

In preparation for the Coronation Futurity, Northern Dancer was entered in the mile-and-seventy-yard Bloordale Purse. Since it is an allowance race, all the horses started with a weight assignment of 122 pounds and were then given weight-reduction allowances according to the terms of the race. Northern Dancer was not given any allowance and carried 122 pounds. Northern Flight carried 117 pounds; Arctic Hills, 115 pounds; and the other four horses, 112 pounds.

Ron Turcotte was back riding Northern Dancer, and this time when the eager colt leaped from the gate, the young jockey steadied him. Another son of Nearctic, Conn Smythe's Northern Flight, soared to a commanding lead. Halfway through the race Northern Dancer was coasting along the rail, third by 15 lengths, and it appeared no one could catch Northern Flight. Then Turcotte moved Northern Dancer out into the centre of the track, and simply let him run. At the top of the stretch, they had drawn up alongside Northern Flight, and down the track they flew, the two sons of Nearctic, duelling stride for stride. At the wire it was Northern Dancer by a length and a half. The other five horses in the Bloordale might as well have been in a separate race. The third-place horse galloped across the finish 25 and a half lengths behind Northern Flight.

12 OCTOBER 1963
WOODBINE RACETRACK

The 51st running of the Coronation Futurity, the richest purse for two-year-olds in the country, attracted a field of 15. According to the conditions of the mile-and-one-eighth race, all colts were to carry 122 pounds, and the three fillies 119. While the *Daily Racing Form* headline suggested that 'Grand Garçon Looms Keen Rival', the fans put their money on Northern Dancer. Once again Turcotte steadied Northern Dancer the instant the colt bounded out of the gate, and sat calmly in fourth place in the early running. This time he allowed the colt to sprint away from the pack a little sooner; halfway through the race they had control.

'This was the last time I rode the Dancer,' said Turcotte, 'and much to Señor Luro's displeasure I just couldn't slow him down to win by less than six or seven lengths, which is why I got taken off him.

'God only knows how good he really was, for he was never a completely sound horse most of the time I rode him, and I still could not slow him down more than that.'

Northern Dancer won the Coronation Futurity by six and a quarter lengths, and with enough reserve to go another lap. Grand Garçon finished a distant fifth.

Northern Dancer was obviously in a league of his own in Canada, so the Windfields planners decided it was time to test him in the United States. The race they chose was the Remsen at Aqueduct in Jamaica, New York (twelve miles from Manhattan), on 27 November.

Northern Dancer's foray into the US, however, was delayed by one more race, the Carleton Stakes at Greenwood – a decision with near disastrous consequences. The original plan was to give him a prep race at Aqueduct before the Remsen, but there appeared to be nothing suitable. The Carleton was chosen, according to Joe Thomas, 'despite the fact he probably would be short, as he hadn't been specifically prepared for the race'.

6 NOVEMBER 1963
GREENWOOD RACETRACK, TORONTO

The races, the racing conditions and the tracks owners or trainers choose are generally a good reflection of the regard they have for a horse.

Established in 1874, and once host to kings and queens, Greenwood in 1963 played only a minor role on the Ontario thoroughbred circuit. The season opened in early spring and closed in late autumn. During summer months, while major races were being contested at Woodbine or Fort Erie, Greenwood was home to standard-bred racing.

When it was first built, the track was located several miles east of the city. By 1963 it was hedged in by homes and shops on three sides, and Lake Ontario on the fourth. Its racing facilities were limited to a single three-quarter-mile (six-furlong) dirt track. (Woodbine's dirt track is a one-mile, or eight-furlong, oval.) Nonetheless, the historic old track was kept operational for more than a century because its urban location made it easily accessible to racing fans. (In 1993, when the Ontario Jockey Club began a major expansion of Woodbine's course, Greenwood was shut down.)

Late in the year Greenwood was cold and damp, undefended against the winter winds that whip across Lake Ontario. On the day of the seven-furlong Carleton Stakes the weather was a cool 52 degrees Fahrenheit and cloudy. There were six horses in the race: Northern Dancer carried 122 pounds, Slithering Sam 117, Northern Flight 115, the other three 113.

As the small field splashed around the muddy track, jockey Jim Fitzsimmons kept Northern Dancer in second place behind front-runner Winkie. When Fitzsimmons sent Northern Dancer to the lead at the top of the stretch, the two horses brushed each other. Northern Dancer won the race by two and a half lengths, but the *Daily Racing Form* described him as 'an unwilling winner, [who] had to be put to strong pressure from Fitzsimmons'. The definition of 'strong pressure' was 'employing the whip from the top of the stretch to the wire'.

When his grooms were bathing off the mud, they noticed blood trickling from the coronet (the sensitive band around the top of the hoof, similar to the quick of a human fingernail). Horatio Luro confirmed it was the beginning of a quarter crack, the same injury that had sidelined Nearctic twice in his four years of racing.

Horses seldom race more than twice in a month. Northern Dancer had run seven races in three months, two under difficult conditions – the boglike course at the Summer Stakes and the muddy Carleton.

Two days after splashing through the mud at Greenwood, Northern Dancer was led up the ramp into the Windfields horse van and sent to the Aqueduct track.

18 NOVEMBER 1963
AQUEDUCT, JAMAICA, NEW YORK

Ten days later Northern Dancer was entered in the Sir Gaylord Purse. Among the seven other entries was Bupers, fresh from his win in one of the premier US two-year-old races, the New York Futurity. Both Northern Dancer and Bupers carried the top weight of 124 pounds. Ridden by Manuel Ycaza, Northern Dancer won the mile race by a decisive eight lengths over Bupers. During the race, however, the quarter crack, a vertical split in the wall of the hoof just below the coronet, became more pronounced.

The wall, or exterior, of the hoof grows downward from the coronet, and is composed of thousands of tiny tubes bound together. The coronet houses papillae, projections that connect to the upper end of each tube, through which secretions necessary for growth travel. If an injury occurs to the papillae, the flow of secretions is interrupted and growth in that area of the hoof stops.

Horatio Luro and Joe Thomas met with the blacksmith to discuss the risks of running Northern Dancer in the Remsen. The consensus was that it was safe, as long as the quarter crack didn't get any worse in the interim. For support, the blacksmith put a special shoe on Northern Dancer's left fore.

The conformation of a horse's feet enable it to run at great speeds over changing terrain. The sole is slightly concave for better purchase, and relatively thin for flexibility. The wedge-shaped frog, extending from the heel and tapering to the centre of the sole, is the first part of the hoof to touch the ground. Like India rubber in consistency, the frog acts as the animal's anti-slipping, shock-absorbing device. In the action of landing and rising, the hoof expands and contracts to adjust to the terrain and absorb the stress.

This expansion and contraction would also deepen Northern Dancer's quarter crack, so a bar shoe was constructed. In this type of horseshoe, a bar of metal joins the two ends, creating a circular band all the way around the bottom of the hoof. This limits the expansion and stabilises the whole foot.

27 NOVEMBER 1963
AQUEDUCT RACETRACK

Northern Dancer leapt smartly out of the gate and went to the lead in the first furlong of the mile-long Remsen Stakes. 'I expected someone else to make a real run at him, but no one did,' said jockey Manuel Ycaza. 'I never cocked my whip, but just tapped him on the shoulder a couple of times at about the three-sixteenth pole and furlong pole. He was running easy.'

Northern Dancer won the Remsen by two lengths; however, the quarter crack had worsened. He would not be the horse to fulfil the Windfields dream of winning the Kentucky Derby. Arrangements were made to bring Northern Dancer back to the farm for a lengthy vacation.

The campaign to determine Northern Dancer's capabilities had come to a halt. In the process, however, the Windfields team had discovered that he had the stuff of champions, including the willingness to push himself beyond his physical limits.

28 NOVEMBER 1963
BELMONT PARK, HEMPSTEAD, NEW YORK

After the Remsen, Luro had Northern Dancer vanned to Belmont Park, where the rest of the horses he was training were stabled. Over the next few days, while waiting for the Windfields van to arrive, he completely changed Northern Dancer's daily routine. Rather than early-morning gallops, the horse had short tours around the stable area with his groom, or he bided his time in his stall.

Not long after they arrived at Belmont, Horatio Luro came upon a magazine article about a trotter called Adios Jr. He, too, had had a quarter crack, but with the aid of a vulcanised patch applied to the injured hoof, Adios Jr. not only resumed training, he won several big races in California.

Luro phoned a friend, the trainer Laz Barrera, in California to find out about the patch. Barrera called back with information and the phone number of Bill Bane, the California blacksmith who had applied the patch to Adios Jr.

Bane explained to Luro that the patch was still experimental and would work only if the quarter crack was in a certain position. Luro sent him detailed photographs of Northern Dancer's left front hoof, and Bane telephoned to say he thought the patch might work. His fee would be $1,000 plus travelling expenses from California.

Luro quickly convinced Taylor of the merits of applying the vulcanised patch. The van that was to collect Northern Dancer and transport him back to Canada was cancelled. The most critical aspect of the experiment was whether Northern Dancer would accept the patch. Horses have highly developed sensory faculties that allow them to perceive danger at great distances. When any of these faculties, but especially the feet, are impaired, the animal will become distressed, for the species depends on flawless, integrated sensory functioning for survival.

Their constantly turning ears operate like radar, detecting sound over long distances. Their feet are acutely receptive sensors that pick up vibrations from the earth, which are then amplified and fed to their inner ears and brains via their nervous systems, bones and body cavities. Thus their entire bodies are one great sound receiver. (This is how horses are able to detect earthquakes and other environmental changes long before their human caretakers.)

Northern Dancer was, of course, a volatile and wilful young stallion. If the experimental patch in any way bothered him, he would likely flail about trying to rid himself of this impediment to his senses, and probably do himself even greater damage.

9 DECEMBER 1963
BELMONT PARK

Early that morning Bill Bane went to work preparing the patch of rubberised material that would bond the crack, yet be flexible enough to feel natural. For the next six hours Bane worked on the material with an acetylene torch to properly vulcanise it – that is, increase its strength and elasticity – before attempting to apply it to Northern Dancer's hoof.

According to Luro, 'Northern Dancer munched at carrots while the application was put in place, and never turned a hair.' Once the patch adhered to the hoof it hardened quickly. Bane suggested they walk Northern Dancer for the following week and then resume training. The patch would simply grow out with the hoof.

Several days later Northern Dancer was loaded into a horse van and taken to the Luro farm in Cartersville, Georgia. There he was turned out daily in a paddock too small for him to get up a head of steam, but big enough for him to wander about, rest up and become accustomed to the patch.

On 22 December 1963, ten days into his Georgia vacation, Northern Dancer was on the road again, headed to Miami's Hialeah Park.

The Rocky Road to the Derby

JANUARY 1964
HIALEAH PARK, MIAMI, FLORIDA

Northern Dancer was back in training, yet it was important to go slowly, so each morning his rider took him for long, leisurely gallops around Hialeah. Northern Dancer had accepted the patch; he wasn't bothered by it nor by the quarter crack. Now that he was no longer in pain, his strength and enthusiasm returned quickly.

Around the back stretch, a champion or potential champion is referred to as the 'big horse', and little Northern Dancer was emerging as the big horse in Luro's shed-row. No one thought he could win the Derby, but he might be a legitimate contender – in itself high praise. Most owners are delighted to have a horse good enough to enter the race: at most twenty horses will be good enough. To qualify, the horses compete in 'prep' races in the months leading up to the Derby. They are like entrance exams: finish in the top twenty money earners and your horse has the opportunity to start in the Kentucky Derby.

In mid-January of each year, owners nominate their best or potentially best three-year-old horses to the US Triple Crown races. The nomination fee is not particularly high ($600 US in 1994) and between 300 and 400 animals will be registered. By the last week in March, the field is narrowed to 25, and the ante to stay in the game raised considerably ($4,500 in 1994). With a month before the Derby, anything can still happen: these élite thoroughbreds, having given their all again and again, are always susceptible to injury. Only 20 horses can run in the Derby; if on the day of the race all 25 final nominees are fit to run, places will be given to the 20 horses with the highest earnings. The owners then pay an entry fee to the

Derby ($10,000 US in 1994) and a starting fee ($10,000 US in 1994).

In January 1964, Northern Dancer was nominated to the US Triple Crown races; Windfields joined several hundred other North American stables daring to indulge in dreams of racing glory.

Most top horses have only one jockey throughout their racing lives, but Northern Dancer had already carried four different jockeys. This precluded any consistency and understanding from developing between horse and rider. When Luro decided it was time to acquire the services of a permanent jockey, he went straight to the top. He called Bill Shoemaker, North America's leading jockey for the seventh consecutive year and winner of two Kentucky Derbys – with Swaps in 1955 and Tommy Lee in 1959. Shoemaker agreed to ride Northern Dancer in several of the prep races, but would not make a commitment for the Triple Crown events.

For Northern Dancer's first prep race, the Windfields team set their sights on the mile-and-one-eighth Flamingo Stakes, on 3 March, at Hialeah. Flamingo winners Citation, Carry Back, Tim Tam, Seattle Slew, and Spectacular Bid all went on to be Derby winners.

The Florida winter had been rainy and the condition of the training track was often less than ideal. Luro didn't want to risk an injury due to poor track conditions, so he occasionally cancelled Northern Dancer's morning workout. As the Flamingo approached, however, Luro decided to enter Northern Dancer in a race to sharpen the colt.

10 FEBRUARY 1964
HIALEAH PARK

Bill Shoemaker wasn't available, so Luro hired Bobby Ussery, Northern Dancer's fifth jockey in ten races. Prior to the six-furlong race Luro instructed Ussery to take it easy, and cautioned him not, under any circumstances, to use his whip.

Six other Flamingo nominees were in the race. Raymond Guest's Chieftain, ridden by Bill Hartack was the favourite, at 11–10. Northern Dancer was the betters' choice for second, at 7–5. Northern Dancer's two-year-old year was far more impressive than Chieftain's, but most of his races had been run in Canada. For many of the handicappers he might as well have been running around Arctic ice floes.

Northern Dancer's 1964 debut was inauspicious. He exploded from the gate, only to be bumped so hard he was knocked off stride and forced to the back of the pack. He regained his balance and advanced steadily along the rail, until he became trapped behind a wall of horses. Forced to slow up, he finished third behind Chieftain and Mom's Request.

In the desperate closing stages of the race Ussery slashed Northern Dancer with his whip. Luro was furious. He publicly denounced Ussery for giving Northern Dancer a bad ride and criticised him for going against his orders.

It was the spring of 1959 all over again, for it was Bobby Ussery who had used his whip on Natalma in the Spinaway at Saratoga. Once again, Windfields' hope of getting to the Kentucky Derby looked about to evaporate.

11 FEBRUARY 1964
HIALEAH PARK

The following morning began like most other days in the Hialeah back stretch. Northern Dancer dug into his feed tub at 6 a.m., washed his meal down with the fresh water in his bucket, and then munched on his hay. An hour or so later he was groomed, saddled and bridled. Luro tossed the exercise rider up on to the colt's saddle and climbed on to his pony to accompany them to the track for a little light exercise.

When they arrived Northern Dancer came to a dead stop. His rider gave him a couple of encouraging boots in the ribs, and Northern Dancer reared straight up and crashed back to the ground. When his rider booted him again, Northern Dancer bucked and lashed out with his powerful hind legs. There was no way Northern Dancer was going to set foot on the track, and no one could force him.

Nature has spared horses the burden of intellectual reasoning; instead they rely on muscle memory: an association with certain situations is stored in their bodies. It is part of the survival mechanism of flight animals, signalling potentially dangerous circumstances and propelling them to bolt. (Yet muscle memory can also work to their detriment: horses often run back into a burning barn not because they have a death wish but because they associate their stalls with safety.)

The sting of Ussery's whip had gone deep: Northern Dancer

associated the track with being whipped, just as his dam, Natalma, had. Northern Dancer, however, was far more volatile and powerful.

Patience seemed the only hope. Every morning for the following week, Northern Dancer was fed, groomed, saddled and bridled. Accompanied by Luro on his pony, he and his exercise rider headed for the track. And every morning, as soon as the track came into view, Northern Dancer stopped dead. Efforts to coerce him to go further made him wild with anger, so they simply walked him up and down the long avenue of pine trees bordering Hialeah's stable area. All future races were on hold.

Luro decided to use the strategy that had won over Natalma. Northern Dancer was given a mild tranquilliser and each morning was toured around the stable area. Gradually he allowed his rider to take him closer and closer to the track. Finally the colt resumed training.

24 FEBRUARY 1964
HIALEAH

Windfields now had to find out if Northern Dancer would actually consent to race. Training was one thing, but they still didn't know whether the energy of the crowd, the walking ring, jogging up the track to the starting gate or the race itself, would trigger an association with the sting of Ussery's whip. Should that happen, there was no predicting how he might react.

Luro chose an exhibition race in which there were only two other horses, Chieftain and Trader, who had been training impressively in South Carolina. He knew that if Northern Dancer was going to get over his disdain for jockeys and whips there was only one person for the job: Bill Shoemaker. At the time, no other rider in North America came close to having his extraordinary reflexes and ability to communicate with horses.

The strategy worked. Shoemaker guided Northern Dancer to a win by seven lengths, in an excellent time of 1:23.4 for seven furlongs.

3 MARCH 1964
HIALEAH PARK

The following weekend Shoemaker rode Northern Dancer in the Flamingo Stakes, which had attracted a field of 11 horses. For most of their owners and trainers, the outcome would indicate whether it was practical to continue aiming for the Derby. The largest crowd of the year gathered for the season première of the most talented young thoroughbreds on the East Coast.

A life-sized bronze statue of Citation presides over the paddock area at Hialeah. To optimistic owners, Citation's presence is appropriate: Citation won the Flamingo on his way to capturing the US Triple Crown in 1948. No horse had taken all three races since then.

Built back in the 1920s, Hialeah echoes the era when wintering in Florida was fashionable for New York socialites – the Whitneys, Vanderbilts and du Ponts – who used to gather on its capacious verandahs as a flock of 450 pink flamingos stalked the banks of the infield lake.

Socialites might no longer spend their winters at Hialeah, but there was a huge crowd, including a number of enthusiastic Canadians, to send Northern Dancer and his popular jockey to the post as the even-money favourites. Northern Dancer catapulted from the starting gate, and Shoemaker settled him in behind Mr Brick, allowing Mr Brick to lead the pack to the top of the stretch. Then Shoemaker simply clucked to Northern Dancer. The horse scorched down the track and won the race decisively, two lengths ahead of Mr Brick. Quadrangle finished third, ten lengths back. His winning time was 1:47.8, eight-tenths of a second off the track record established by Bold Ruler in 1953.

It was a great day for the Canadian racing fans, especially Winifred Taylor, who had flown to Miami from the Bahamas for the race and who accepted the trophy. Her husband missed the entire event. Fog at the Toronto airport delayed his flight so long that by the time he arrived at Hialeah, Northern Dancer was back resting in his stall.

Northern Dancer's Flamingo victory indicated that he had recovered from his racetrack anxiety and was fit and eager to race. Barring further problems, he was on the road to the Kentucky Derby.

That evening Northern Dancer received a telegram c/o Horatio Luro, from California: 'ROSES ARE RED STOP VIOLETS ARE BLUE STOP IF I HAVE MY WAY I'LL RUN PAST YOU STOP SIGNED HILL RISE.'

8 MARCH 1964
GULFSTREAM PARK, NORTH MIAMI, FLORIDA

In preparation for his next major race, the Florida Derby on 4 April, Northern Dancer was entered in a seven-furlong event. Shoemaker had a prior commitment, so Manuel Ycaza rode the horse.

Northern Dancer sailed around the oval course in a track record time of 1:22.4 and won by four lengths. In second place was another Kentucky Derby candidate, The Scoundrel, carrying eight pounds less than Northern Dancer.

3 APRIL 1964
GULFSTREAM PARK

On the morning before the Florida Derby, Luro planned on giving Northern Dancer one last good tune-up, but what was meant to be, in racetrack jargon, a mild 'blow-out' erupted in a severe blow-up.

Northern Dancer's regular exercise rider, Ramón Hernandez, was in Toronto, so a substitute rider was called in. (Northern Dancer was not an easy horse to ride, and it seems curious to switch exercise riders the day before a major event, but that's apparently what happened.)

The rider's instructions were to gallop a half mile in an easy 48 seconds, but Northern Dancer had his own agenda. Feeling fit, strong, and ready to race, he grabbed the bit and took off; his rider was helpless. When he finally got Northern Dancer under control, they had covered five furlongs in a blistering 58.6 seconds.

Northern Dancer had run his race – a day early. Running him in the Florida Derby now was like asking him to race on two consecutive days. It seemed impossible that any horse could have the physical reserves to repeat the performance the following afternoon.

4 APRIL 1964
GULFSTREAM PARK

As the horses headed for the starting gate the Windfields team held little hope of Northern Dancer winning the Florida Derby. The optimistic fans, however, declared him their overwhelming favourite at 3–10.

Northern Dancer was quick out of the gate, but as the horses converged into the first turn, he was mid-pack, with no running room. Shoemaker simply kept Northern Dancer close to the rail and bided his time. By the final turn, the front runners had faded, and Northern Dancer was in the lead, with Shoemaker sitting quietly, never using his whip. They coasted to a one-length victory over The Scoundrel. The time for the mile and an eighth was a leisurely 1:50.8, no small accomplishment, considering that Northern Dancer had virtually run back-to-back races. It was remarkable that he'd had the stamina to run, let alone win.

There was no doubt now among the Windfields team that Northern Dancer was on his way to the Kentucky Derby, yet the US racing press continued to be sceptical of his chances.

The *Thoroughbred Record* stated: 'Oddly enough, the chief reaction to Northern Dancer's victory in the Florida Derby seems to be speculation that he will lose some other race [the Derby] in the future . . . While the Dancer's victory was obviously decisive and the runner-up had no excuse, I think The Scoundrel might be more troublesome when they have another furlong to go [as in the Derby].'

Daily Racing Form columnist Joe Hirsch reported: 'It did not appear that Shoemaker had a lot of horse left at the wire.'

Art Grace at the *Blood-Horse* was one of the few journalists to buck the tide: 'The Scoundrel wasn't going to catch Northern Dancer if they had gone around the track twice more.'

Oblivious to the controversy, one tired Northern Dancer was back at the stables, attacking his food with a vengeance. The floor of his stall was covered in a thick layer of peat moss, as a substitute for his straw bedding, which he had begun to eat. His already voracious appetite had been stimulated by training and racing. He was devouring twice what most racehorses consume, but still found room for the straw, which wasn't particularly nutritious.

His handlers also celebrated with a dinner, but it became a sombre affair when Bill Shoemaker announced he would not be riding Northern Dancer in the Kentucky Derby. He explained that he had been offered both The Scoundrel and Hill Rise, and he was putting his money on Hill Rise.

Although later Shoemaker called his decision a 'terrible bonehead call', Northern Dancer's detractors saw it as further evidence that the Canadian colt had no chance of winning the Derby. After all, the country's leading jockey had rejected Northern Dancer for Hill Rise, the outstanding three-year-old on the West Coast.

'I watched Hill Rise run on several occasions at Santa Anita last winter,' Shoemaker explained, 'and was very impressed with him. Northern Dancer is a fine colt and I am deeply grateful to Mr Taylor and Horatio Luro for the opportunity of having ridden him. However, my instincts tell me that Hill Rise is the better mount for the Derby, and I hope I am right.'

Interestingly, a year and a half earlier Horatio Luro had had the chance to train Hill Rise. In 1962, Decidedly, the colt Luro had trained for Californian George Pope, won the Kentucky Derby in record time. When Luro was back at Santa Anita that winter, Pope asked him if he would take one of his two-year-olds with him on the East Coast circuit the following spring. Luro agreed and chose a colt that showed a lot of speed.

Several days later Pope's horse van arrived at Luro's Santa Anita stable area. Down the ramp came a big, handsome, long-legged colt, but it was not the horse Luro had selected. That colt had bruised his foot, so an alternative, Hill Rise, was sent. After working with Hill Rise for a few days, Luro called Pope to say that racing this colt in the spring would be premature; Hill Rise needed more time to develop. He was sending him back to Pope's ranch.

Luro was right: Hill Rise didn't even start racing until almost year-end. A magnificent-looking animal, he developed into a brilliant racehorse. He won his first start on 22 November 1963, and was on a seven-race winning streak, including a six-length triumph in the premier Kentucky Derby qualifying test on the West Coast, the Santa Anita Derby.

With Bill Shoemaker committed to riding Hill Rise, Luro immediately telephoned Bill Hartack, the jockey who had ridden Decidedly in the 1962 Derby, his third Derby win. Hartack agreed to ride Northern Dancer in the Blue Grass Stakes at Kentucky's Keeneland racecourse, prior to the Derby; barring any problems, he might ride the colt in the Derby.

Bill Hartack was a particularly outspoken and opinionated jockey. Arrogant and sarcastic, he lashed out at trainers and spat insults at the media. Even though Luro was one of the few trainers he respected, Hartack was capable of stomping off and leaving Northern Dancer riderless yet again.

6 APRIL 1964
GULFSTREAM PARK

Northern Dancer had now given his handlers and owners passes to a very exclusive club. As the horses wintering in Florida made their way back to Woodbine and Belmont and various home bases, Northern Dancer and his excited crew made plans for Kentucky.

In preparation for the trip, Northern Dancer's legs, from his ankles to just below his knees, were protected by large sheets of cotton gauze wrapped with three-inch-wide bandage, similar to a tensor bandage. His hay was stuffed into a loosely webbed haynet and tied within easy munching distance in his stall in the horse van. Water buckets, feed tubs, pitchforks, horse blankets, a tack trunk and extra hay were stored in the front of the van. When everything was loaded Northern Dancer was walked up the ramp and secured in his stall.

The road trip from Gulfstream to Keeneland is about 1,200 miles – a long distance to be on your feet, even if you have four of them. The horse van stopped at Luro's Georgia farm for several days to break the journey.

10 APRIL 1964
KEENELAND RACETRACK, LEXINGTON, KENTUCKY

Northern Dancer handled the long trip to Keeneland well. One of the few rural tracks in North America, Keeneland is like a health spa for horses, in the heart of Blue Grass Country. Beyond its boundaries miles of white board fences criss-cross the rolling green pastures. For Northern Dancer and the other new arrivals, Keeneland's pastoral atmosphere was a refreshing change from urban tracks. The crisp, clear spring air was particularly invigorating for horses coming from the heat of Florida.

Built in the 1930s on a section of John Keene's Keeneland Stud Farm on the outskirts of Lexington, the track reflects Kentucky's proud horse-racing history, which dates back several centuries. Giant trees flank the long lane leading to the ivy-covered buildings, flower gardens and the tree-shaded walking ring.

Hill Rise, shipped by air from California, was already settled in by the time Northern Dancer arrived at Keeneland. They would not meet, however, until Derby Day. For his final Derby tune-up Hill

Rise was entered in the Forerunner Purse on 17 April. (With Bill Shoemaker in the saddle, Hill Rise scored his eighth consecutive victory in this seven-furlong sprint.)

Northern Dancer was scheduled to run in the Blue Grass Stakes, the featured event of Keeneland's spring meet. The race is a mile and an eighth – a furlong less than the Derby – and is run nine days before the Derby.

Not everyone agreed that Hartack should be riding Northern Dancer. When Joe Thomas suggested in a newspaper interview, just days before the Blue Grass, that he thought Hartack was not the best rider for the horse, the controversy became public. 'I am running the stable!' Luro fumed in the next edition.

23 APRIL 1964
KEENELAND RACETRACK

Early on the morning of the Blue Grass, while Northern Dancer was eating his breakfast, staff at Kentucky's other horse farms hurried through their chores to get to Keeneland in time to catch a look at the speedy little Canadian challenger.

Each horse in the race had its own walking ring, and a huge crowd closed in around Northern Dancer. As people jostled for a better view, Northern Dancer held his head high, scanning the sea of gawking faces.

The crowd favoured Northern Dancer to win the five-horse race at 4–5 odds. Northern Dancer bolted out of the gate and would have taken immediate command of the race had Hartack not kept him back. Royal Shuck plodded in the lead, while Northern Dancer galloped grudgingly alongside.

Coming into the stretch, Hartack eased his grip a little and Northern Dancer coasted into the lead. Suddenly the Kentucky-bred Allen Adair brought the Kentucky fans to their feet as he charged out of the pack. Hartack glanced over his shoulder, loosened his grip a bit more, and Northern Dancer crossed the finish a half length ahead of Allen Adair. Rather than pulling Northern Dancer up at the wire, Hartack sent him an extra furlong, the Derby distance. The time was 2:03, compared with Decidedly's 1962 record of 2:00.4. The handicappers decided Northern Dancer was not up to the classic distance. Hill Rise seemed a much better bet.

The Kentucky Derby

25 APRIL 1964
CHURCHILL DOWNS, LOUISVILLE, KENTUCKY

Northern Dancer was led down the short ramp of the horse trailer and into his stall in Barn 24. Although the distance between the two tracks is only about seventy miles, Churchill Downs is a world apart from the elegant and spacious Keeneland.

The 48 barns, rambling grandstand, one-mile dirt track, seven-eighths-mile turf course, grooms' quarters, offices, maintenance buildings, parking lot and Kentucky Derby Museum are crammed into 140 acres. (Canada's Woodbine, by contrast, is 773 acres.) It sits like an island, with a sea of homes, shops, service stations and factories crushing against its boundaries.

Beneath prominent twin spires, the stands amble alongside the home stretch and around the clubhouse turn in a higgledy-piggledy manner. The first of the grandstand buildings was constructed in 1895 and, as the Derby grew in popularity, additions were made here and there, in a variety of architectural styles. Its gingerbread ornate mouldings, carved eaves, curly cornices and balconies of varying shapes and sizes produce a refreshingly eclectic effect.

Churchill Downs may not have the conveniences of modern tracks or the charm of Keeneland and Saratoga, but it does have dignity and character. In anticipation of the annual Derby pilgrimage, each spring Churchill Downs gets a facelift. Yet another coat of paint is applied to the white clapboard and green trim; the hardwood floors are buffed, cobblestones swept and flower gardens pruned.

The Kentucky Derby, fashioned after Britain's Epsom Derby, was conceived to showcase Kentucky's thoroughbreds, and Churchill Downs was built specifically to host the race. An estimated 10,000

Kentuckians came out to the new track to witness Aristides win the first Kentucky Derby on 17 May 1875.

The Derby quickly became the highlight of the Kentucky racing and social season, but by the turn of the century Churchill Downs was losing money and about to close down, taking the fledgling Derby with it. Then along came a portly, cigar-chomping Louisville promoter, Colonel Matt Winn. In 1902, Winn and a group of investors bought Churchill Downs, and the track – and the Derby – became his lifelong passion.

Winn set out to lure North America's best thoroughbreds to the Derby; however, the big East Coast stables saw no reason to travel to Kentucky for a parochial little race. Winn decided to give them a new perspective: the Kentucky Derby, he declared, was a contest between the best three-year-olds in the East and West. (It was really a contest between the best thoroughbreds east and west of Lexington, but that didn't hamper his sales pitch.)

It wasn't long before he had a receptive audience in the press: Damon Runyon, Grantland Rice, and other colourful and powerful newspaper columnists. The flamboyant Winn wined them and dined them; they reciprocated by writing lavishly about the Kentucky Derby. When Old Rosebud won the race in 1914, Grantland Rice coined the phrase 'the run for the roses'.

The following year the filly Regret won the Kentucky Derby. Her owner, Harry Payne Whitney, declared, 'I don't care if she ever wins another race, or if she even starts in another race. She has won the greatest race in North America!'

A win for the prominent New York-based Whitney stable, and with a filly, made headlines across the country. Whitney's words 'the greatest race in North America' were quoted over and over by Winn's journalist friends. Winn took it one step further and dubbed the race 'the greatest two minutes in sport'. Yet it wasn't until 15 years after the colonel's death that Northern Dancer became the first horse to run 'the greatest two minutes' in two minutes.

The Derby seemed to reciprocate by providing the media with stories laced with drama: two jockeys slashing each other with their crops as their horses galloped neck and neck to the wire; Native Dancer's only defeat in 22 races; Bill Shoemaker thinking he had the race won on Gallant Man and pulling up at the infield pagoda instead of the finish, then the horse's owner telling the media he had dreamed this was going to happen.

And, this year, Northern Dancer would carry on the tradition of giving the media plenty to write about.

28 APRIL 1964
CHURCHILL DOWNS

In the final days before the Derby, Northern Dancer was in peak condition, as evidenced by the way he bounced out for his sunrise gallops around the historic track. Keeping him calm and relaxed was never easy, but at the Derby there was a complicating factor: the dawn patrol. A media army – in 1994 there were 1,200 accredited print, radio and television representatives – arrived at the stable area early in the morning in search of a story. For many of the troops it's the only horse race they attend, let alone cover, all year. Not knowing a fetlock from a forelock, they gravitate toward the obvious. And the little horse from Canada was obviously a story.

Luro gave groom Bill Brevard most of the credit for keeping Northern Dancer calm under the barrage. Brevard was a 'valuable ally . . . his placid manner, love of a good horse and sense of responsibility made him an ideal partner'.

An endless procession of photographers converged on Barn 24, asking that Northern Dancer be taken out of his stall for a photo. Concerned about the additional pressure and chaos, Luro devised a wily solution. Few of the photographers, he knew, would recognise any of the Derby horses, let alone Northern Dancer; all they knew about him was that he was small. Luro used his own lead pony as a photo double for Northern Dancer. The pony was a chestnut and bore no resemblance to Northern Dancer, but no one seemed to notice.

Later in the day, the fans at Churchill Downs got their first look at Hill Rise, and they liked what they saw. The California champion and Bill Shoemaker flew to a two-and-a-quarter-length victory in the Derby Trial Stakes. Five horses, including Citation and Dark Star, the only horse ever to defeat Native Dancer, had won the Derby Trial and gone on to win the Derby. The consensus at Churchill Downs was that by the end of the week, a sixth horse would be added to the list, and that was Hill Rise, the Derby favourite. Northern Dancer was picked to finish second – David to Hill Rise's Goliath.

1 MAY 1964
CHURCHILL DOWNS

Northern Dancer set out for his final early-morning workout before the big race. He started out slowly and was clocked at 24.4 seconds for the first quarter; he ran five furlongs in 1:00.4, and galloped out six furlongs in 1:14. The hands of exercise rider Raymond Cerda were red and stinging from trying to restrain the colt; Northern Dancer was ready to run.

Following the workout, Horatio Luro joined the other Derby trainers, officials, owners and media in the racing secretary's office to draw post positions for the next day's race.

The name of each horse in the field was printed on a card and placed in a box. As trainer of a recent Derby winner, Luro was given the honour of reaching into the box and pulling out the cards one by one. The horses were listed in the order they were chosen.

At 10 a.m. sharp, 12 numbered ivory balls were dropped into a leather-covered bottle. The racing secretary shook the bottle and tipped it on its side so the ivory balls would roll out one by one. The order in which they appeared would determine the post positions.

Depending on the number of horses in the field, the length of the race and the racecourse itself, post positions can play a significant role in the outcome. On North America's oval courses, usually three or four positions from the rail is considered prime. Horses assigned post positions close to the rail can run into traffic problems, since the field converges towards the rail as they approach the first turn. Horses starting out furthest from the rail have the disadvantage of being forced to cover more ground.

At Churchill Downs, however, a slight majority of Kentucky Derby winners had come from the number-one post position, next to the rail; positions two, five and ten followed.

Mr Brick, the speed horse Northern Dancer defeated in the Flamingo Stakes, drew the rail. Hill Rise was assigned post position 11. When it came to Northern Dancer's name on the list, ivory ball number 7 rolled out of the leather-covered bottle. Position 7 was in the middle in the 12-horse field. Luro seemed pleased.

2 MAY 1964
CHURCHILL DOWNS

By 7 a.m. Northern Dancer had devoured every single oat Bill Brevard had put into his feed tub and was scanning his stall for his hay, his usual next course. There wasn't any: his first clue that this was a race day.

'He knows,' Brevard explained to a Toronto reporter standing outside the stall. 'When he doesn't get any hay, it must be a racing day.'

Horses have delicate digestive systems. Before a race, trainers reduce their usual amount of food to avoid any cramping that might result from running on a full stomach. Creatures of habit, they soon identify any change in their routine, and what it implies.

A small breakfast was not the only indication that something was happening: the atmosphere in the back stretch at Churchill Downs was different. Things appeared unusually calm. The dawn patrol had dwindled to a mere handful. The behind-the-scenes interviews had been wrapped up; the big story was now the race. Grooms went about their early-morning chores quietly, methodically, with little of the normal banter. Trainers ambled about: there was nothing they could do but wait.

After Northern Dancer had finished his breakfast, Bill Brevard slowly brushed the colt's hide until his bay coat gleamed. He and Luro checked every inch of Northern Dancer's compact body, then Brevard casually walked the colt around the stable area for an hour, before returning him to his stall.

At mid-morning the blacksmith inspected Northern Dancer's light aluminium horseshoes to ensure that they were nailed tightly to his hooves. Shortly thereafter, Brevard dumped a large tin of oats into Northern Dancer's feed tub. After this light lunch, Brevard braided the colt's short black mane, which made him appear more than usually small and compact. He didn't look like a challenger of the finest thoroughbreds in North America, but like an entrant in a Pony Club competition.

A few hundred yards away from Barn 24 the infield was filled with crowds armed with picnic baskets, blankets, lawn chairs and drink coolers. They had been pouring into the infield since 8 a.m. The sky was overcast, but the temperature was in the mid-70s Fahrenheit and the party was in full swing. (Many of the thousands packed into the Churchill Downs infield would not catch a glimpse of a horse all day – and not care.)

Hawkers were winding their way through the crowd, selling Kentucky Derby souvenir glasses containing the official Derby drink: the mint julep.

Kentucky Derby Festival had been in full swing for more than a week now – on the streets, in the parks, and in the homes and gardens of Louisville. There were steamboat races, balloon races, lawn parties, black-tie dinners, Kentucky Colonel barbecues, concerts, luncheons and the annual Pegasus Parade. With each passing day, the excitement had built and built in anticipation of the grand finale.

While those in the infield party were in casual picnic attire, clubhouse patrons and box holders, the famous and would-be famous, had dressed for the occasion: celebrities in designer originals, Southern-belle costumes complete with parasol, and otherwise conservative dress topped with a papier-mâché hat in the shape of the twin-spired grandstand. On Derby Day, it seems, anything goes.

At the conclusion of the sixth race the 11 Derby contenders were led by their grooms from the back stretch to the paddock on the far side of the stands. Bill Brevard guided Northern Dancer to saddling stall 7, then stood at his head, patting him and talking to him. Huge crowds gathered outside the paddock area, straining to see the horses.

When the bugler sounded the call to the post, Luro tossed Bill Hartack up into Northern Dancer's saddle. E.P. and Winifred Taylor held hands as they watched Hartack, in their Windfields turquoise-and-gold silks, on their volatile colt, while the band in the infield played 'The Star-Spangled Banner'.

When Mr Brick led the parade on to the track the band struck up 'My Old Kentucky Home' and the hundred thousand fans began to sing. Northern Dancer unleashed a fierce buck.

Once on the track Northern Dancer seemed to settle down, although he did look impudent. And small – he was four inches shorter than almost every other horse in the field. Ahead of him in the procession were Mr Brick, The Scoundrel and the impressive-looking Quadrangle. A few horses behind him was the magnificent Hill Rise. Tall, his neck arched, he glided effortlessly over the dirt track. His eyes were large and bright, his coat coal black.

The six horses ahead of Northern Dancer walked willingly, one by one, into their starting stalls, but when it was his turn, Northern Dancer had no intention of co-operating. The minute the gate-crew member took hold of Northern Dancer's bridle to escort him into the stall, the colt bolted backwards, dragging the fellow with him. Most of the 100,000 fans, who had put down their mint juleps just long enough to place their wagers on Hill Rise, watched the defiant Northern Dancer with little more than passing interest. But the Taylors and the thousand or so Canadians there to cheer on 'the Dancer' were aghast: if Northern Dancer decided he wasn't going, a platoon of Mounties couldn't get him in that gate. Then, just as suddenly as he had balked, Northern Dancer strolled into the stall. The Canadian sigh of relief was palpable.

The publicity and debate over Northern Dancer's chances, reported daily from Kentucky by a half-dozen Canadian journalists, piqued interest and enthusiasm back home. We had begun to believe we had a chance, albeit a remote one, of winning and, perhaps more significant, proving the American experts wrong.

In any case, on that overcast first Saturday in May 1964, millions of Canadians, the majority of whom had never been to a racetrack, settled in front of a television to cheer on the Dancer.

In the starting gate, Northern Dancer stood patiently as the remainder of the field were secured in their stalls. Seconds after the last horse, Roman Brother, was led in, the bell clanged, the stall doors flew open, and the field was charging down the track.

Past the stands, the outside horses moved toward the rail in anticipation of the first turn. Northern Dancer was on the rail, sitting seventh, with ample running room in front of him. Hartack continued to restrain him, and kept him on the rail as they ran around the bend and into the back stretch.

As the field charged into the final turn Northern Dancer was still on the rail, trapped by a solid wall of horses: Hartack's strategy had backfired. Northern Dancer had easily caught the front runners, and now had no place to run. Any hope of cutting around them was dashed by Hill Rise, thundering alongside, like a predator keeping his quarry hemmed in.

Suddenly Northern Dancer shot sideways, right under Hill Rise's chin, and blazed around the front runners. His neck stretched full out, and his short, choppy stride was so fast his legs were a blur. When Shoemaker realised what had happened, he quickly rode Hill

Rise in pursuit, but it took several seconds for the lanky horse to get into gear.

Once he got rolling, Hill Rise chased Northern Dancer with a vengeance, gaining ground with each long, powerful stride. It seemed impossible that little Northern Dancer, straining with every short, choppy stride, could stave off the mighty Hill Rise.

Like a highway-patrol car, Hill Rise caught up to the Canadian speedster and drew alongside. His head was at Northern Dancer's hind quarters, then at his flanks. Mere yards from the finish Northern Dancer must have felt Hill Rise's hot breath on his shoulder, and stretched his neck even further. As the horses flew across the line it was Northern Dancer by a neck! And a new track record of two minutes flat!

In that instant Northern Dancer became 'our' horse. Canadians poured into the streets to celebrate. Car horns honked, total strangers patted one another on the back. His victory was our victory, and we basked in the triumph he had given us.

Northern Dancer had not only waltzed off with America's greatest horse-race title, but had sprinted around Churchill Downs track faster than any horse in the Derby's illustrious 90-year history.

Northern Dancer's victory was front-page news across Canada: 'From the grandstand packed with Kentuckians who bred 70 of the previous 89 winners, a new sound rose over the din of the 100,000 fans on the grounds. It came from five Canadians who stood proudly and let one verse of "O Canada" rise out of their hearts, as their hands clutched enough tickets on the winner to paper a wall,' wrote former managing editor of the *Toronto Star*, Ray Timson.

Canadian journalist Trent Frayne was also among the carload of sports writers who had driven to Louisville for the event.

'But now from the roof of the ancient grandstand where I was standing (and, I realised, screaming),' wrote Frayne in *Northern Dancer and Friends*, 'it became apparent that Hill Rise's advance had stopped, that Northern Dancer was fighting him off. There were still many strides to the wire, but Hill Rise was stopped there, his snout at Northern Dancer's neck. The little horse had his head thrust out in that driving style of his, and nothing was going to stop him.

'I found myself pounding my fists repeatedly on to a restraining railing there on the roof, and shouting over and over, "He's going to make it! He's going to make it! He's going to make it!"

'And of course he did.'

Northern Dancer's Final Races

4 MAY 1964
PIMLICO RACETRACK, BALTIMORE, MARYLAND

Northern Dancer arrived at noon and immediately began fussing about his new stall, looking for food. He was a little weary from the 14-hour van ride, but his colossal appetite was unaffected. Most of the fans were still unconvinced that he was a better horse than Hill Rise, and the California champion was the early favourite to win the Preakness Stakes, the second US Triple Crown race.

The betters may have been ignoring Northern Dancer, but the US State Department and Pentagon weren't. Northern Dancer would, as sportswriter Red Smith put it, inspire 'the first military invasion of the United States since the War of 1812 when British troops won the gratitude of architects everywhere by burning the White House in Washington.'

Pimlico publicity director Joe Hickey had contacted the Ontario Jockey Club to arrange for a ceremonial guard from the Governor-General's Horse Guards to participate in the Preakness festivities. Hickey had seen the troop in Toronto, where they form the honour guard for the Royal Family or their representatives during the ceremonial ride around Woodbine's track in a horse-drawn landau on Queen's Plate day.

The Governor-General's Horse Guards is the oldest unit of the Canadian militia. When horses gave way to tanks and bombers, the regiment retained a mounted troop, which trots through the twentieth century as a ceremonial unit. The members are volunteers – butchers, bakers, and barristers – and their horses are borrowed from the Pony Club. As an invading force they pose no great threat, although the predecessor of the Guards did participate in the 1812 troubles. When Pimlico proudly announced they were coming to the Preakness, someone leapt to attention and produced a Canada–United States treaty, drawn up following the War of 1812, prohibiting armed military units from crossing the shared border.

The Guards' ceremonial accoutrements include shiny but dull-edged swords, lances and a large silver axe, carried by the farrier-sergeant. Although times had changed, the treaty had not: the swords, lances and axe made the Guards an armed military unit. Before you could say 'the British are coming', the State Department, External Affairs, Canada's ambassador to the United States and the Pentagon had become involved. Eventually peace was declared, and five members of the Governor-General's Horse Guards and their horses received temporary permission to enter the United States of America.

16 MAY 1964
PIMLICO RACETRACK

Consensus around 'Old Hilltop', as Pimlico has been called for a century, was that the Kentucky Derby had depleted Northern Dancer's strength and stamina; he would not be able to defeat Hill Rise a second time. On the morning of the Preakness, Pimlico's track handicapper declared Hill Rise the favourite at 7–5; Northern Dancer was second at 2–1. The Scoundrel was quoted at 4–1, Quadrangle and Roman Brother at 8–1. Big Pete, a sprinter, was the long shot at 20–1. By the time the six-horse field galloped to the starting gate the crowd was strongly behind Hill Rise, at odds of 4–5.

Hill Rise certainly appeared ready to avenge his Derby defeat. In the post parade he pranced proudly, his aristocratic head held high. A light sweat gave his black coat a deep sheen. Northern Dancer merely strolled along, his head low. Yet when the starting bell clanged, Northern Dancer exploded from the gate. Jockey Bill Hartack had to restrain the colt to keep him in third place. No one wanted to take the early lead. The strategy appeared to be to conserve the horses in the first part of the race. The outsider Big Pete loped along in front – and the first quarter was clocked in a leisurely 25.2 seconds. Then the threesome of Northern Dancer, Quadrangle and Hill Rise increased the pace, tearing down the track almost abreast. At the half-mile pole Northern Dancer sprinted free.

On the turn to home, Hill Rise attempted to challenge Northern Dancer, but his reserves were spent. At the eighth (mile) pole, with three-sixteenths of a mile to go, a wearying Hill Rise was three lengths off Northern Dancer's pace.

Northern Dancer streaked across the finish, an easy victor. Two and a half lengths behind, Hill Rise was locked in a duel with The Scoundrel for second: The Scoundrel beat him by a head.

When E.P. Taylor walked out to the infield to accept the Woodlawn Vase, the Preakness trophy, the five Governor-General's Horse Guards trotted down the track and formed an honour guard behind Taylor as he raised the trophy in front of the cheering crowd.

By the time Northern Dancer was settled back in his stall in Pimlico's back stretch, and no doubt looking for something to eat, he was the centre of yet another controversy. At the victory party in Pimlico's Members Club, E.P. Taylor was no doubt taken aback when Horatio Luro declared he did not intend to run Northern Dancer in the Belmont, the third race in the US Triple Crown. The announcement itself was stunning, but his taking this stand in public, without consulting Taylor, was even more astonishing.

Luro told his audience that Northern Dancer had 'distance limitations', that the mile-and-a-half Belmont would be too much for him. The following morning, however, Taylor met with Luro. Northern Dancer would be shipped to New York: the decision to run at Belmont would rest solely on whether the colt was physically fit.

Luro's bombshell fuelled a new round of speculation. According to the *Toronto Star*'s Milt Dunnell, 'Mr Taylor had lunched with the Queen during a recent visit to England . . . She congratulated Mr Taylor on Northern Dancer's victory in the Derby . . . One US writer in the press box cracked: "She told him to go for three." So the Belmont is a command performance.'

The sceptics were beginning to see the light: 'Northern Dancer converted the die-hards to believers that he is the master of Hill Rise and any other three-year-old this season,' wrote Joe Kelly of the *Washington Star*.

'Northern Dancer is too much horse,' said Hill Rise's jockey Bill Shoemaker after the Preakness. 'He's just the best and that's all.'

Quadrangle's jockey, Braulio Baeza, spoke for the Preakness field. 'We all have one big trouble. The big trouble is that we could not keep up with that Canadian. We could not handle him. Other than that my horse had no trouble.'

Bill Boniface of the *Baltimore Sun* wrote: 'Owners and trainers of the East's classic-calibre three-year-olds will be darned glad when . . . Northern Dancer goes back to Canada.'

18 MAY 1964

The Monday following the Preakness, Northern Dancer climbed aboard the waiting horse van. Destination: Belmont Park. The Belmont Stakes was being run at Aqueduct while Belmont's new grandstand was being built. (The old one had become a firetrap and was closed down in 1962. Construction was completed in 1968.) Luro, however, had stalls and a cottage at Belmont Park, which he used as his training base on the East Coast.

Northern Dancer continued his daily workouts and appeared to be in good physical condition. 'Luro began to think that perhaps he was wrong and that the husky little Canadian colt might actually stay the 12 furlongs of the Belmont,' wrote Joe Hirsch in *The Grand Señor*.

The Belmont Stakes is considered the most demanding of the US Triple Crown races. The third classic race in seven weeks, it is also the longest. Stamina is critical, and many horses that enter the Derby simply don't have the physical reserves to carry them through all three races.

In the previous 45 years there had been only eight Triple Crown winners, and none since Citation in 1948. In 1963, Chateaugay had come close, winning the Derby and the Belmont, but he was second in the Preakness. In 1961, the popular Carry Back won the first two, but, in one of the most surprising upsets in the history of the Belmont, he finished seventh.

Now it was Northern Dancer's turn to try to win all three races.

6 JUNE 1964
AQUEDUCT RACETRACK, JAMAICA, NEW YORK

Grey clouds hovered over Aqueduct's massive grandstand. In spite of the rain forecast a large crowd had assembled to witness Northern Dancer run in the Belmont and perhaps into racing history. Finally he was, at 4–5, the favourite. Almost everyone wanted him to win, it seemed.

But he didn't win.

His blazing trademark stretch run wasn't there and he finished third to horses he had left standing on many other occasions. Luro's instructions were to keep Northern Dancer in check, behind the early leaders. The pace was exceptionally slow and Hartack kept a strong hold on the reins as Northern Dancer strained at the bit. So much dirt was thrown up from the heels of the pace setters that for two hours after the race Northern Dancer spat and coughed up dirt.

The disappointing outcome led many to conclude Northern Dancer wasn't up to the challenge: New York's *Sports Inquirer* ran a red banner headline that read 'Northern Dancer Quits'. Charles Hatton of the *Daily Racing Form* wrote: 'On the basis of Saturday's race . . . Northern Dancer does not stay.'

There were those, including E.P. Taylor, who were convinced Bill Hartack misjudged the pace and kept Northern Dancer under severe restraint far too long. Some blamed Luro for instructing Hartack to hold Northern Dancer back in the early part of the race. Others believed that both Luro and Hartack underestimated the capabilities of the horse.

The only certainty was that the tendon problem that would terminate Northern Dancer's brief career after his next race began in the Belmont.

14 JUNE 1964
WOODBINE RACETRACK, TORONTO, ONTARIO

Northern Dancer walked down the ramp of the large red-and-white horse van, led by Bill Brevard, who had travelled home with him from New York. An enthusiastic crowd of grooms, trainers, reporters and track employees had gathered to welcome home the conquering hero.

Although there was a buzz of excitement, the reception was a far cry from the one Toronto mayor Alan Lamport had planned. His idea was to host a massive ticker-tape parade down Bay Street, the heart of the city's financial district. When Taylor explained that Northern Dancer, like any highly strung thoroughbred, would not be able to handle the chaos of the parade, Lamport instead declared Monday, 8 June 1964, Northern Dancer Day in Toronto. A civic reception was held in his honour at city hall, and he was awarded the key to the city – this one carved out of a carrot. E.P. Taylor

Northern Dancer (Michael Burns)

Lady Angela (Michael Burns)

Nearctic (Michael Burns)

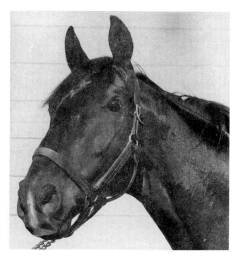

Natalma (Michael Burns)

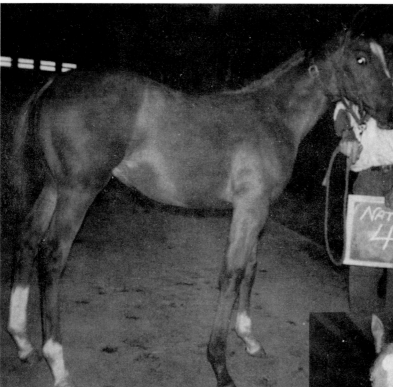

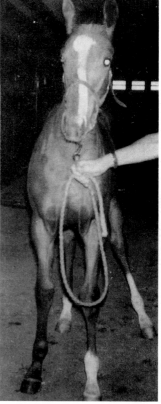

*October 1961. Northern Dancer's
thoroughbred foal registration application.*
(Courtesy The Jockey Club)

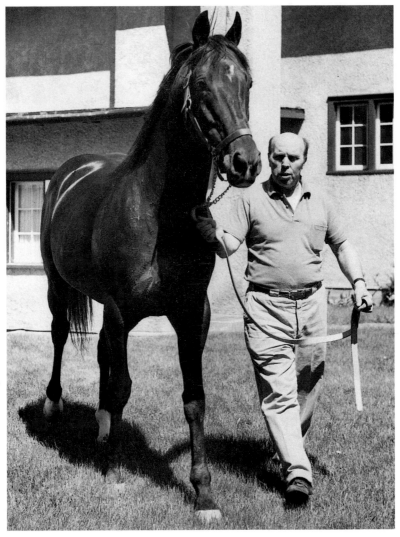

July 1963. Nearctic and his 'guardian angel', Windfields stallion manager Harry Green (Michael Burns)

Opposite: *2 August 1963. Northern Dancer wins his first race by eight lengths. 'But it could just as easily have been ten or fifteen,' says his jockey, Ron Turcotte* (Michael Burns)

April 1964. After an arduous and muddled Florida campaign, Northern Dancer is at Keeneland for the Blue Grass Stakes, his final Derby prep race (Toronto Star)

Opposite top: 2 May 1964. Northern Dancer thunders past the Kentucky Derby finishing post in a record two minutes flat (Michael Burns)

Opposite bottom: 'This is a great day for Canada!' beams E.P. Taylor, standing with his colt in Churchill Downs winners' circle. The jockey is Bill Hartack (Michael Burns)

16 May 1964. Northern Dancer scorches to an easy victory in the Preakness Stakes (Michael Burns)

Opposite: *Displaying the Preakness trophy, E.P. Taylor is joined by members of the Governor General's Horse Guards* (Michael Burns)

14 June 1964. Northern Dancer returns to Canada to run in the Queen's Plate. Led by his groom, Bill Brevard, he stretches his legs after the long journey from New York (Toronto Star)

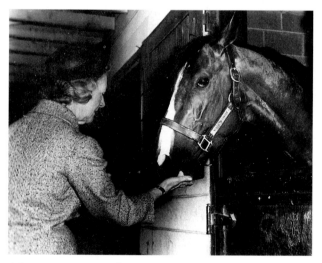

16 June 1964. Northern Dancer had a legion of fans, but his greatest admirer, from the time he was a foal, was Winifred Taylor (Michael Burns)

20 June 1964. Clearly in a class of his own. Northern Dancer wins the Queen's Plate by seven and a half lengths (Michael Burns)

En route to the Queen's Plate winners' circle, Winifred Taylor chats to Northern Dancer with (left to right) *Bill Brevard, Bill Hartack and E.P. Taylor* (Michael Burns)

September 1968. Nijinsky, the magnificent son of Northern Dancer and Flaming Page, at the Canadian Thoroughbred Horse Society Yearling Sale. He was bought by American Charles Engelhard and sent to Vincent O'Brien's Ballydoyle Stud in Ireland (Michael Burns)

Opposite: 27 October 1964. The Queen's Plate is Northern Dancer's last race. The tendons of his left foreleg, injured in the Belmont, are now critically strained. He is retired to the National Stud Farm north of Oshawa, Ontario (Toronto Star)

Viceregal (Michael Burns)

Below left: *The Minstrel* (Michael Burns)
Below right: *Nureyev*

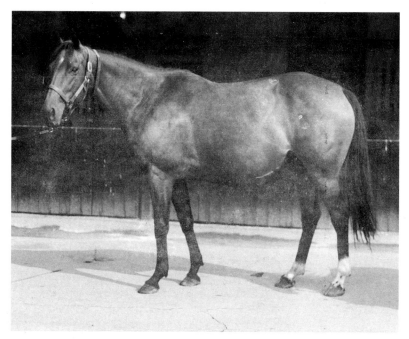

25 June 1977. Fanfreluche, in foal to Secretariat, was kidnapped from Claiborne (Pierre Levesque)

16 November 1990. Northern Dancer died and was buried at Windfields Farm, midway between the barn where he was born and the barn where he began his days as a stallion (Bernard McCormack)

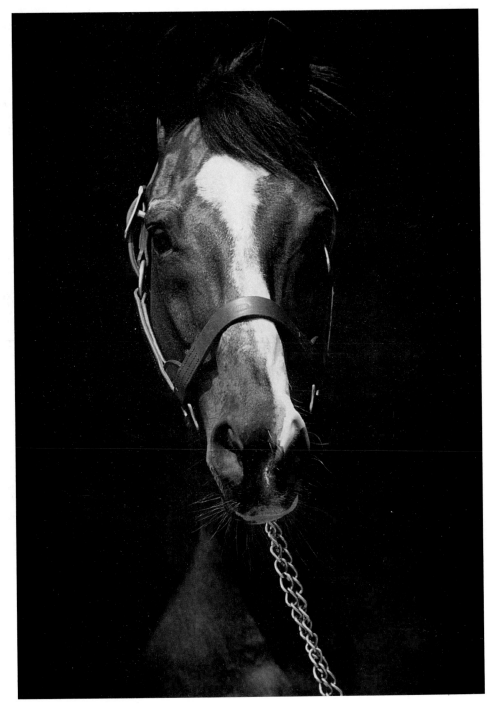

Northern Dancer (Doug Sanders)

accepted the key on Northern Dancer's behalf, stored it in his refrigerator, and presented it to the horse shortly after he arrived at Woodbine. Northern Dancer enthusiastically ate the key in one chomp.

Sacks of Northern Dancer fan mail from across Canada, the United States and the Bahamas were arriving at the Windfields office, a small house on the corner of the estate. Taylor's executive assistant, Beth Heriot, headed up the operation to respond to all Northern Dancer's fans. With the help of Mr and Mrs Taylor, all the letters and requests for a photograph of the horse were answered.

'I am 8. I will be in the fourth grade. I love your Northern Dancer. I have saved every picture of Northern Dancer I can get. But none are very good. Would you please send me a good picture?' (from Kentucky)

'I am 12 years old and I just love Northern Dancer . . . Would you please send me a picture of Northern Dancer so that I can hang it in my bedroom? P.S. My mom says it is silly to write this letter.' (from Toronto)

An autograph collector in New Brunswick asked for a copy of Northern Dancer's hoofprint. Others asked for one of his shoes. Then there were all those two-dollar bills that arrived in the mail with a request that Taylor bet for them the next time Northern Dancer ran. (The money was returned.)

A woman in British Columbia sent Northern Dancer a four-leaf clover, another offered oil leases in Utah in exchange for a Northern Dancer offspring. People sent pencil drawings and paintings of the horse, poems and essays and birthday cards and, when he didn't win the Belmont, condolences.

One of Northern Dancer's many fan letters was from a young student from the Brantford School for the Blind, who had written to ask if he could meet Northern Dancer and possibly pat him. Winifred Taylor wrote back that she would be pleased to introduce them.

Mrs Taylor's fondness for the horse, from the time he was a foal, appeared to be reciprocated by Northern Dancer. (Once, when he was standing at stud in Maryland, she paid him a visit. The staff asked if she wanted them to bring him out of the stall. 'No,' she replied, 'I'll simply go in with him.' Within seconds Northern Dancer had grabbed her by the wrist and, to the horror of the staff, he began walking around the stall with her. He could easily have broken her wrist. But Mrs Taylor remained calm, and eventually he delivered her back to the stall door. She thanked him for the tour.)

When Mrs Taylor and the 13-year-old blind boy arrived at Woodbine, Northern Dancer was resting in his stall. His ears perked at the sound of a familiar voice and he stretched his neck over the barricade of nylon webbing and peered down the shed-row. The familiar voice, of course, belonged to Winifred Taylor. She was standing three stalls away, speaking with Horatio Luro. Northern Dancer lowered his head and nickered.

Luro was apprehensive about Mrs Taylor's promise to the blind boy. Not long before, he had fled Northern Dancer's stall when the volatile young stallion had turned on him. There was no telling what Northern Dancer might do.

Yet as Mrs Taylor approached him, Northern Dancer relaxed and lowered his head to her. He was uncharacteristically docile as she patted and spoke to him about her young guest and his letter. Then, slowly and gently, she guided the blind boy's hand to Northern Dancer's nose. And as long as the youngster patted him, Northern Dancer stood as quiet as an old cart-horse.

Northern Dancer had struck a chord in the hearts of Canadians from coast to coast. British Columbia lumberjacks, Alberta cattle ranchers, prairie farmers, Bay Street stockbrokers, Québécois bakers, maritime fishermen, First Nations council members, women, men and children shared a common bond.

Yet it is not surprising that we were united in our admiration of Northern Dancer. Horses are an integral part of Canadian heritage. Thoroughbred racing in Canada evolved from contests held in the tiny British garrison towns and fortresses along the St Lawrence River and the Great Lakes. The flat grassy plain around Niagara's Fort George provided a perfect turf course, and by the late-1700s, three-day race meets had become great social occasions, complete with festive dinners, raucous parties and dancing till dawn.

Horses, of course, were basic transportation for everyone from General Brock to the local doctor. Since only two horses are required to constitute a race, early contests were often a spontaneous affair: each zealous owner put up a stake, and the winner took all. The necessary straight stretch of road frequently turned out to be the main street of town, much to the detriment of pedestrians. Eventually, in the interests of public safety, race areas were relegated to the outskirts of the villages. Over time, small grandstands were built on these properties, and Canada had her first racetracks.

Generally considered a pastime of the local gentry, Canadian racing had barely enough rules to regulate an event. Turf Club committees were ill-equipped to deal with the larceny of professional gamblers.

Cheating was the norm. Frequently the lead handicapping weights disappeared from saddle pads during a race and mysteriously reappeared just before the jockey weighed in at its conclusion. Horses, too, disappeared, only to resurface with new identities, and sometimes new colours. Moreover, the first horse to the wire was not always the winner if the racing officials were given sufficient monetary incentive to reverse their ruling.

The Queen's Plate, Canada's most prestigious horse race – and the oldest annual horse race in North America – was run for the first time in 1836 at Trois-Rivières, then a small village, on the St Lawrence River. Conducted under royal patronage, it was called the King's Plate, after King William IV, the reigning British monarch.

In 1859, the Toronto Turf Club petitioned his successor, Queen Victoria, to similarly honour thoroughbred racing in Canada West (Ontario). Queen Victoria granted the request and split the annual purse of 100 guineas between the two events. On the afternoon of 27 June 1860, what would become the Queen's Plate was first held at the racecourse in the village of Carleton, four and a half miles north west of Toronto. Four thousand fans – in coaches, sulkies, buggies and on foot – made the trek along the dusty, twisting road.

The president of the Toronto Turf Club, Colonel Casimir Gzowski, fired the starter's pistol, and the field of eight horses bolted down the track in the first of three one-mile heats. As the horses dashed past the judges' stand, jockey Nelson Littlefield flew off his mount, Paris, and came crashing to the ground, where he lay still as death before the horrified crowd. Suddenly he bounced back to his feet, and the relieved fans were free to return their attention to the race. The horse Bob Marshall had won by half a length over the favourite, Don Juan. After a 15-minute respite, the horses were off and running in the second heat. This time Littlefield, apparently recovered from his tumble, was aboard Don Juan. The switch proved advantageous, and Don Juan beat Bob Marshall by several lengths. In the final heat, Littlefield and Don Juan defeated Bob Marshall once again.

During the next 20 years the Queen's Plate was staged in towns and villages across Ontario, seldom without incident. In Hamilton, a brawl among a group of firemen spilled out on to the track across from the judges' stand. The mêlée was interrupted briefly when one of the participants was run over by a racehorse. Two years later the Plate was delayed until a unit of mounted hussars cleared the track of rowdy spectators.

Gzowski and other Turf Club directors were certainly trying to hold legitimate races worthy of royal patronage, but many of the spectators viewed the annual Plate as an opportunity for drinking, gambling and having a brawling good time.

'Outside the stands,' observed the *Toronto Daily Leader*, following the 1861 Plate, 'were the gambling gentlemen, the now-you-see-it-now-you-don't class, who dupe the thoughtless innocent and the foolhardy adventurers overburdened with dollars. Dice appeared to be the favourite game.'

In 1881, a retired publican and the owner of Woodbine racecourse, Joseph Duggan, and Toronto's postmaster, T.C. Patteson, persuaded Casimir Gzowski, now aide-de-camp to Queen Victoria, to join them in forming the Ontario Jockey Club. Their mandate was to 'put down all nefarious practices with a strong hand, and to establish such a discipline as would include owners, trainers, jockeys and the betting fraternity'.

Two years later, Gzowski invited his house guests, the Marquess of Lorne, Governor-General of Canada, and his wife, Princess Louise, daughter of Queen Victoria, to attend the Queen's Plate. The marquess returned to England with the recommendation to the Queen, no doubt encouraged by Gzowski, that the horse race needed a permanent home. Queen Victoria agreed, and the race has been held in Toronto, under the auspices of the Ontario Jockey Club, ever since.

20 JUNE 1964
WOODBINE RACETRACK

As Northern Dancer was led up the chute toward the saddling enclosure for the 105th running of the Queen's Plate, hundreds of fans crowded the fence to catch a glimpse of him. Many of them had never been to Woodbine or even bet on a horse race, but they were here to cheer Northern Dancer. And cheer him they did.

When Northern Dancer stepped on to the track, announcer Daryl Wells managed only '. . . and number 2 is Northern . . .' before his words were drowned in the roar of applause.

Six colts and one filly were set to challenge Northern Dancer. The crowd, however, was backing Northern Dancer; his final odds were 1–7, a pay-off of 15 cents for each dollar wagered. Thousands of the tickets on Northern Dancer were never cashed, but kept as souvenirs.

When the eight-horse field thundered past the grandstand for the first time Northern Dancer was running second last, tightly held by Bill Hartack and boxed in against the rail by Canadian Oaks winner, the filly Later Mel. The entire crowd was on their feet. Would the Plate be a repeat of the Belmont? Or worse?

Galloping around the clubhouse turn, Northern Dancer was running dead last. Surely he didn't deserve to be beaten, not like this. Something had to be dreadfully wrong.

Hartack's post-race explanation for this heart-stopping moment was that his horse was running faster under a stranglehold than the others in full flight. 'I tried to take him back of the whole field so we could get out,' said Hartack, 'but I couldn't get him slowed down enough, so I was forced to go through the first opening I saw.'

There really wasn't an opening, to his right and only feet ahead was Later Mel; on the rail was the lumbering Return Trip. Hartack slackened his hold on Northern Dancer's reins, and the sheer force of his charge created an opening. Finally unrestrained, he flew down the back stretch, blasting between Later Mel and Return Trip, past All Seasons and Pierlou, then Top Ruler, Grand Garçon and Langcrest.

The entire crowd was screaming wildly, 'Come on, Dancer! Come on, Dancer!' And didn't stop until Northern Dancer sailed across the finish seven and a half lengths ahead of second-placed Langcrest, another son of Nearctic, and twelve lengths ahead of Grand Garçon, the colt that had edged out Northern Dancer in the Cup and Saucer the previous year.

Northern Dancer won the Queen's Plate on sheer heart. He had run four classic races in the previous month and a half, and his left foreleg, strained in the Belmont, was now bothering him signi-ficantly. Northern Dancer had really run, and won, the Queen's Plate on three legs. But it would be his last race.

Athlete of the Year and
Soon-to-be Sire of the Century

27 OCTOBER 1964
NATIONAL STUD FARM, OSHAWA, ONTARIO

Northern Dancer steadied himself in the back of the van as the lumbering tractor-trailer negotiated the turn through the stone pillars into the National Stud Farm. The air was crisp and cool. The autumn leaves of the ancient oak and maple trees that lined the lane were a brilliant kaleidoscope of colour. Horses grazed lazily in the paddocks on either side of the road. Giant salmon in the river that winds through the forest behind the riding arena were fighting the rapids in their annual migration.

The van eased to a halt in front of the large stallion barn, where Harry Green was waiting to show Northern Dancer to his spacious stall. Northern Dancer had returned home to stay.

The tendons of his left foreleg were critically strained. Further racing might have resulted in irreparable damage, especially since Northern Dancer had shown himself willing to run in spite of pain.

Tendon sprains usually occur at the gallop, and the horse most susceptible is the thoroughbred racehorse. The sprain doesn't happen early in the gallop or during a race in which the horse is fit and strong, but when fatigue sets in. When the muscles lose their resilience the stress is borne by the tendons, which are inelastic and unable to cope. Initially the sprain appears as a slight swelling that can be symptomatic of a number of problems. If, after treatment, the swelling persists, all work with the animal must desist, since more exercise may cause the tendon to rupture.

Watching the film footage of the Belmont, one can easily see how and when Northern Dancer's injury set in. Hartack's tight hold would have been enervating, especially considering Northern Dancer's aggressive nature. Then there was the mud and dirt kicked up in his face: horses of his calibre, driven to be at the head of the pack, can become angry under those circumstances. For the first part of the race Northern Dancer, his neck bowed, was galloping up off the ground instead of forward, as horse and rider fought each other. When Hartack finally let him go, Northern Dancer's energy had been spent; his famous acceleration simply wasn't there. Fatigue had set in, as had the first stages of his injury.

Whether Northern Dancer won or lost the Belmont is insignificant. His fans were disappointed, and winning the US Triple Crown would have enhanced his value when he entered stud, but what matters is that because he didn't win the mile-and-a-half Belmont, many people in the business concluded that he couldn't – or wouldn't – go the distance. They assumed his offspring would likely be fine sprinters, not distance horses. So Northern Dancer's years as a stallion began as his racing days had: with the experts sceptical.

Taylor had delayed retiring Northern Dancer because, as the Kentucky Derby winner, the horse had been invited to run in the thirteenth annual Washington DC International. To be held on 11 November, the Washington International, at the Laurel track, was one of the most prestigious races on the continent. The Canadian (now Rothmans Ltd) International and the Washington International were the only North American races focused on bringing European and British horses to challenge the top North American horses. Also invited to the 1964 Washington race were Santa Claus, winner of the Epsom Derby; French Derby winner Le Fabuleux; and several national turf champions.

Taylor had hoped that if Northern Dancer had the opportunity to go up against and beat the best horses in the world, no one would doubt his little horse ever again. But in the end he decided it wasn't worth the risk to the horse's vulnerable left foreleg: on 6 November 1964, he announced Northern Dancer's retirement. Commencing in 1965, Northern Dancer would be available for stallion duties for a fee of $10,000 (live foal).

Immediately Taylor received proposals from leading US breeders either to syndicate Northern Dancer or to have him stand at stud at one of their big breeding farms. But Taylor declined all offers. His rationale was summed up in the following reply to an offer from Kentucky:

> I am particularly grateful to you for the enthusiasm you showed for this horse [Northern Dancer] and for giving me practically *carte blanche* in regard to terms and conditions if I were to let you syndicate or manage him.
>
> You will appreciate that I found it very hard in many ways to come to the decision I finally reached. As you may imagine, financial considerations were not uppermost in my mind. The real reason is that I simply want the horse here and I know that the multitude of his admirers in Canada would misinterpret my motives if I were to send him away – I trust you will understand.

By the time the announcement was made public, Northern Dancer's book was already full. Taylor planned to send ten of his best mares to Northern Dancer. The remaining mares were to come from North America's top thoroughbred breeders, most of them in Kentucky: Claiborne Farm, Greentree Stud, Hermitage Farm, Jonabell Farm, Manchester Farm and Spendthrift. Mrs Richard C. du Pont and Harry Love would ship their mares from Maryland. Pennsylvania's Hugh Grant and Virginia's Nydrie Stud, Newstead Farm and Keswick Stables also booked mares. So did Canadians Max Bell, Bill Beasley, Larkin Maloney and George Gardiner.

Northern Dancer settled into his new life with ease and put on a bit of weight. His gypsy existence – long van rides that led to strange and new tracks, early-morning gallops, the excitement of the races and the roar of the crowd – was a thing of the past. His days were now taken up with eating, sleeping, ambling about his stall and patrolling his large paddock at the west side of the barn.

14 NOVEMBER 1964

The *Daily Racing Form* pollsters unanimously declared Northern Dancer the Best Three-year-old and Horse of the Year in Canada. First, however, they had to rewrite the competition rules. When Horse of the Year honours were first given out back in 1951, the only criteria were that the horse be foaled in Canada and that it do its best performing in Canada. The award thus reflected Canadian racing at the time, since, apart from the Taylors' Victoria Park, Windfields, Natalma and Nearctic, few Canadian-bred thoroughbreds were sent south of the border by their Canadian owners.

To shape the top award to fit its celebrated recipient-to-be, the requirement that the horse do its best running in Canada was dropped. The *Racing Form* added three new categories – Best Three-year-old, Best Juvenile and Best Older Horse.

The Older Horse honour was awarded to an animal that closely shared Northern Dancer's lineage, but not his destiny. His name was E. Day and his sire was Empire Day, the foal Lady Angela so desperately tried to protect in the hold of the ship when rescued by Harry Green. E. Day was a four-year-old campaigner whose only recognition was indignation from the fans when he didn't win. In 1964, E. Day had won at distances ranging from six furlongs to a mile and a sixteenth and had finished in the money in several mile-and-a-quarter races. Earlier in his career, E. Day had been kicked around in $2,500 claiming races, and somewhere along the line one of his owners had had him gelded.

3 DECEMBER 1964

E.P. and Winifred Taylor attended the annual Thoroughbred Racir.g Association dinner to accept the Best Three-year-old of the Year award on behalf of Northern Dancer. The judges, racing secretaries from across the US, chose Kelso Horse of the Year for the fifth consecutive year. Now seven years old, Kelso had won more money than any other horse.

At the end of December Northern Dancer won an award no horse has ever won before or since. Canada's leading sports editors and journalists benched thirty or so humans and named Northern Dancer Athlete of the Year.

It was an Olympic year and Northern Dancer was up against some impressive Canadian athletes: track stars Bill Crothers and Harry Jerome; gold-medal rowers Roger Jackson and George Hungerford; silver judo medallist Doug Rogers; Canada's gold-medal bobsled team; hockey players Jean Beliveau, Charlie Hodge, Stan Mikita and Gordie Howe; football players Tom Brown and Tommy Grant; boxer George Chuvalo; and jockey Ron Turcotte.

Not everyone was pleased with this extraordinary tribute to Northern Dancer. Russ Taylor of radio station CFCF in Montreal, a supporter of Bill Crothers, was outraged that the award went to 'a beast'. Most Canadians, however, agreed with the choice, and it wasn't long before driving out to Windfields Farm to see Northern Dancer became a regular family outing. Every weekend so many Canadians flooded the farm that visiting hours had to be suspended temporarily because of the chaos and congestion.

FEBRUARY 1965
NATIONAL STUD FARM

Northern Dancer was waiting impatiently on a cold and grey February morning for Harry Green to lead him outside. Ever since he had arrived back at the farm, each day was much like the one before: Harry and his assistant arrived 6.30 a.m. and the stallions were fed and turned out in their individual paddocks. On this day, however, Harry had not taken Northern Dancer out.

Northern Dancer's obsession with food in his racing days had been replaced by a yearning to be outdoors, free to roam. No matter how deep the snow or how severe the cold, outside was where he wanted to be. A disruption in his schedule made Northern Dancer anxious and angry.

Finally, at about 10 a.m., Harry arrived at the volatile stallion's stall. Northern Dancer reared up, slammed his right hoof on the floor, and glared at Harry through the stall bars.

Harry approached him cautiously. Once he won Northern Dancer's confidence (and no doubt regained his own), he clipped the lead shank on Northern Dancer's halter, and led him out into the wide aisle. Out in the cold, blustery air Northern Dancer bounced and bucked happily. Instead of going to the paddock, however, they headed down the path toward the indoor arena. Northern Dancer was about to breed – or attempt to breed – his first mare, Flaming Page.

Flaming Page had been chosen with good reason: she was an exceptional racehorse, the best filly bred in Canada yet. (For students of divination, Flaming Page was also the seventh foal of the mare Flaring Top, and from the seventh crop of the stallion Bull Page.)

As a yearling, she was the filly Frank Sherman had bought at the 1960 Windfields sale, then exchanged when he noticed she had an inflamed fetlock. This one act altered the history of the thoroughbred, since it is unlikely that Sherman or any Canadian other than Taylor would have raced her in the US, thereby proving her superiority as a racehorse. Canadian owners, at the time, were content to race their horses in Canada. To most of them, racing was recreation, a respite from hectic corporate empires. They enjoyed watching their horses run, but for the most part saw little need to race elsewhere. Taylor, by contrast, had a mission.

It is also unlikely that Sherman, owner of a small racing stable, would have bred Flaming Page to Northern Dancer. Yet Flaming Page became the dam of Nijinsky, and the grandam of The Minstrel, the two sons of Northern Dancer that set off the buying frenzy for Northern Dancer offspring.

Flaming Page was a late bloomer. She didn't begin her two-year-old year until early September and got in only a few races before the end of the Canadian racing season. At three, however, the long-striding filly made her presence known. In the US she ran against three-time champion Cicada, the tough little speedster who in forty-one races was out of the money only four times and won her owners close to $800,000 – a world record for a filly. Flaming Page finished fourth to Cicada in the Oaks Prep Stakes at Churchill Downs and second to her in the Kentucky Oaks. Flaming Page gave Canadian racing fans a demonstration of her brilliance and stamina when she returned to win the Canadian Oaks, and a week later trounced the country's top colts in the Queen's Plate.

Equally important, Flaming Page was tall, nearly a full hand taller than Northern Dancer. While there could be no doubt now that Northern Dancer was exceptional, people continued to see his height as a problem. No one wanted foals to be built like him (not yet, at least). By matching Northern Dancer with Flaming Page, it was hoped that the foal might have Flaming Page's height and body type.

Halfway down the path to the indoor arena Northern Dancer began to sense Flaming Page, and that she was in season. Once he was inside the arena, Harry could hardly restrain him, but there was a serious logistical problem. Try as he might, Northern Dancer was simply too short, and Flaming Page got so fed up she kicked him smack in the ribs.

'A very scientific solution was found,' Peter Poole, the Windfields farm manager, said, laughing.

Poole had his staff dig a shallow pit in the centre of the arena's dirt floor for the mare to stand in. They poured a concrete base, surfaced it with asphalt, and blanketed the entire area with nonslip matting. Northern Dancer was then able to consummate his relationship with Flaming Page. Unfortunately the result of this breeding was stillborn twins.

Northern Dancer took to his new vocation with enthusiasm. Such was his commitment that he was prepared to service each and every one of the more than one hundred mares on the property. Much to his displeasure, he had to share stallion duties with eight others, including his own sire, Nearctic.

From early on, Northern Dancer had shown an extremely strong biological urge for fillies and mares. At the track, when a filly or mare was in the vicinity, his attention was immediately diverted. This, coupled with his already unpredictable and volatile nature, had led Luro to suggest that Northern Dancer be castrated. Luro had argued that the colt would be calmer and more manageable with his focus on training and racing, rather than the opposite sex.

Taylor said no. He had acquiesced to a similar request from Luro several years earlier, and regretted the decision. In 1961, Taylor bought a yearling son of Ribot, which he named Roman Flare. Half-brother to the successful sire Nantallah, the colt was purchased as a potential stallion.

Apparently Roman Flare's temperament made him difficult for Luro to train. Like Northern Dancer, Roman Flare often lost his concentration when there were fillies in the vicinity. Luro convinced Taylor that only as a gelding would Roman Flare reach his full racehorse potential. Instead, Roman Flare ended his racing career as a $1,500 claimer.

Stud colts, particularly those that are highly sexually charged, can be not only difficult to work with, but dangerous: perhaps nature's way of assuring survival of the species is to make the genetically superior stallions more combative, more aggressive. In the wild, each herd has only one stallion. He achieves his status with his superior strength and stamina and will fight to maintain it. In theory, he will also pass on this strength and stamina to his offspring.

A herd stallion is always vulnerable to the challenge of younger stallions. At about a year old, once they can fend for themselves, the colts leave the main herd and join the other males. They will practise fighting, like young gladiators, preparing for the day they will battle to win their own herd.

When another stallion was led past Northern Dancer's stall *en route* to the arena to breed a mare, Northern Dancer flew into a rage. Rearing, bucking, hollering and slamming around his stall, he kicked over water buckets and demolished feed tubs. The problem was that Northern Dancer considered all the mares on the farm to be part of his herd, and as such, was prepared to breed each and every one of them. The sight of another stallion going toward the breeding arena made him crazed. Putting him out in his paddock wasn't the answer – he would simply gallop himself into a lather and possibly get hurt.

Finally, the crew at the farm resorted to tying him up in his stall in these stressful situations. Since he had shown he could snap the strongest hemp, they secured him with a thick metal chain. They looped the chain around one of the vertical metal bars at the front of his stall and clipped it to the metal ring of his halter, under his chin. Confident this would do the trick, Harry Green, Peter Poole, and the crew dispersed to tend to their other farm duties. Seconds after they left the barn they were startled by a crash from the direction of Northern Dancer's stall. When they returned to the stallion barn, the astonished horsemen found Northern Dancer hanging upside down by the chain. It seems that, chain or no chain, Northern Dancer was still determined to get to the breeding arena and had attempted an escape over the top of the partition. When they unclipped the chain he fell to the ground with a great thud.

That first season, however, he danced and pranced his way down the path to the arena to breed a total of 35 mares. Later veterinary examinations found 26 of the mares to be in foal. The following spring, there were ten sons and daughters of Northern Dancer romping about the fields of the National Stud Farm. Eleven others were foaled elsewhere.

Northern Dancer's legacy had begun.

PART THREE
Northern Dancer's Legacy

The thoroughbred exists because its selection depended not on experts, technicians or zoologists, but on a piece of wood: the winning post of the Epsom Derby. If you base your criteria on anything else you will get something else, not the thoroughbred . . . the conditions of the Derby have remained unchanged and its validity unquestioned; it is the Epsom Derby which has made the thoroughbred what it is today.

Federico Tesio

Northern Dancer's return to the National Stud Farm not only symbolised fulfilment of the dream to raise a Kentucky Derby winner on the farm's abundant pastures, it proved to be a turning point in the history of the thoroughbred.

Northern Dancer stood at the vertex between the past and the future of racing and breeding. He was born of the past – a young man's passion for thoroughbreds and an old man's wish that his beloved farm not be destroyed by real-estate developers.

He emerged from an age in which owning thoroughbreds was an expensive hobby and great fortunes were spent maintaining the horses and stables. Yet Northern Dancer played the pivotal role in changing the thoroughbred game to one in which horses were a commodity more valuable than gold, and in which the new breed of owner set out to make vast fortunes from these animals.

It was during the mid-1970s that the focus shifted from spending fortunes on horses to making fortunes on horses. Money was in ample supply, and the players in this new game were looking for a return on investment. They put their money on Northern Dancer. By some mystery of nature, he was inordinately prepotent. At the time there were 7,000 thoroughbred stallions at stud in the US alone, yet none rivalled Northern Dancer as a sire of winners and champions.

Thoroughbred breeding does not subscribe to artificial insemination. When Northern Dancer stopped breeding, that would be it: none of his sperm would be frozen for future use.

The run on the limited number of Northern Dancer offspring became so outrageous that Northern Dancer's value as a stallion eventually far surpassed any possible dollar value.

It was as if humanity's age-old love affair with the horse had taken a quantum leap into the bizarre. As the passion escalated, thoroughbred racing shifted from sport to big business. Outcomes of the yearling sales were analysed and reported in the Wall Street Journal. It must have been confusing for market analysts accustomed to more commonplace commodities: spending millions on thoroughbred babies made no sense, since the horses could never win back anywhere near their owner's investment. There was no guarantee that these expensive horses would get to the racetrack, much less win a race.

It didn't matter. Not only did Northern Dancer sire exceptional racehorses, he passed on his genetic supremacy. Many of his offspring proved to be sires and dams of yet another generation of great champions.

Owners may have paid millions for Northern Dancer yearlings, but a number of the colts were syndicated for up to ten times the original investment. And in the process, the structure and destiny of thoroughbred racing changed drastically.

How Northern Dancer became the central figure in all this is not unlike how he came to be in the first place – a succession of twists of fate. Yet he would not have had such an important role in this drama if he had not been so extraordinary, and had he not passed on his power, magic, and the will to win to so many of his offspring.

Northern Dancer sired 635 foals: of the 80 per cent (511) that started in races, 80 per cent were winners; 146 horses were stakes winners. Twenty-six of these animals were champions in Great Britain, Ireland, France, Italy, the United States or Canada.

Heading the list of champions was the first foal sired by Northern Dancer.

The Magnificent Dancers

Northern Dancer could have had no more appropriate first-born than the magnificent Viceregal. Heir to his sire's tremendous will to win, Viceregal was also one of the most beautiful thoroughbreds to step on to a racetrack. He looked every inch an aristocrat. When the sun touched his chestnut coat it gleamed like gold. His eye was kind and generous, yet before a race it burned with the 'look of eagles'. A blaze of white from his forelock to his nostrils accented his perfectly sculpted features. When he pranced on to the track his hooves seemed barely to touch the ground.

Viceregal's stakes-winning dam, Victoria Regina, was a half sister to Victoria Park. Her lineage traced back through the generations to Windfields' foundation mares and stallions.

Several weeks prior to the annual sale of yearlings, Viceregal's groom went to the paddock to fetch the colt back to the barn. Viceregal was waiting for him at the gate, standing on three legs. His left foreleg was swollen above the ankle. There was a good chance Viceregal would miss the sale.

That year, 1967, the Windfields event was special, at least in E.P. Taylor's eyes, for it included the first crop of Northern Dancer foals. This called for a revision of the sale's format. Previously, when more than one person was interested in the same horse, he wrote their names on slips of paper, put them in his cashmere cap, and had someone draw the winner. For this sale he had hired professionals: auctioneer Laddie Dance and announcer John Finney from the New York horse-auctioning company Fasig-Tipton. All the horses still carried fixed prices, but if two or more parties were interested in a horse, the auctioneer would open up the bidding at the set price. Preferred buyers – those who had purchased yearlings in previous years – made their selections and purchases ten days before the yearlings were offered to the general public.

Viceregal's sprain did not appear to be serious, and by sale time he was no longer lame, but his ankle was still puffy and neither the preferred buyers nor the general public buyers were interested in him. Later that autumn he joined the other Windfields colts and fillies to be trained by Pete McCann.

Although Viceregal possessed the will and the exceptional talent to run, his ankle continued to be troublesome. Nonetheless, time and again Pete brought this magnificent son of Northern Dancer to the starting gate in peak condition.

In 1968, two-year-old Viceregal was undefeated in eight starts, seven of them stakes races. (During this time, however, his right foreleg started to give him trouble.) On 6 October 1968, in the Cup and Saucer Stakes at Woodbine, it appeared that Viceregal was going to suffer his first defeat. Coming into the home stretch, he was a good ten lengths behind the leaders. Suddenly he became almost airborne, his golden mane flying in the wind and his long tail sailing behind like a banner. He galloped across the finish a neck ahead of the unsuspecting front runner, Grey Whiz.

It's impossible to know what propelled Viceregal that mild October afternoon; whatever it was that carried him to victory despite his physical limitations and his pain abandoned him in the winner's circle. Viceregal limped away lame. His already vulnerable ankles had taken a severe beating. He had clipped himself several times on the inside of his fetlock and the hoof of another horse had struck him on the outside. Viceregal was immediately shipped back to the farm, where he would be under the constant care of the staff and resident veterinarian.

All eyes were on the majestic son of Northern Dancer when he made his debut as a three-year-old in the six-furlong Whitney Purse at Keeneland on 5 April 1969. It was hoped he would prove the next Canadian-bred challenger in the Kentucky Derby.

When he jogged on to the track Viceregal seemed to have recovered fully. Muscles rippling beneath his shining chestnut coat, head held high, he looked every inch a champion.

Distracted by the sight of a fallen jockey, Viceregal got off to a slow start, but he soon settled in. Coming into the home stretch, he was bounding easily, but he flattened out in the final yards of the race. He finished third, a creditable effort for his first race of the year. But it would be his last. No sooner had Viceregal crossed the finishing line than jockey Craig Perret jumped off. Viceregal was limping.

'When I saw the boy rein him up past the finishing line and dismount,' recalled Taylor, 'my heart jumped to my throat.'

The courageous Viceregal had finished third on what was diagnosed as a fractured coffin bone in his left fore.

Kent Hollingsworth, editor of the *Blood-Horse*, summed up Viceregal's final race in an article entitled 'Another Good One Tries Too Hard', this way: 'The really good ones, driven by competitiveness and courage, try beyond their physical limits, where lesser hearts withhold for another week.'

Northern Dancer sired 21 foals in his first year at stud. Although Viceregal was by far the most beautiful and exciting, his other offspring also proved themselves racehorses of substance.

The first of Northern Dancer's progeny to enter a race was Jitterbug, a filly owned by Greentree Stables. She won a three-furlong dash at Hialeah on 26 January 1968. Two months later the second starter, True North, a colt that C.V. Whitney bought at the Saratoga sales, broke the 22-year track record for four and a half furlongs at Santa Anita.

There is a span of three years between the time a stallion breeds a mare and the time when the two-year-old offspring begin racing. Moreover, since the most important races are for three-year-olds, owners and syndicate members must wait four years to discover whether a stallion has passed on his genes and produced superior foals, or will not make it as a stallion at all. There is no technical or scientific way of knowing. Many top racehorses have failed to sire comparable animals.

But Northern Dancer was off to a good start. Of his first crop of 21 foals, 18 were runners, 16 were winners, and 10 of the 16 were, remarkably, stakes winners. (Stakes winners are the cream of the crop. In North America less than 4 per cent of all races are designated as stakes.) As a rule, fewer than half the thoroughbreds born start a race; of those only one quarter (12.5 per cent of the total) will win in their first season. Thus Northern Dancer's statistics (76.2 per cent winners) was six times the average success rate.

For the market breeders, those who sell their yearlings at public auction, Northern Dancer also appeared to be a good investment. In 1967, seven Northern Dancer yearlings were sold at the sales at Saratoga and Keeneland. All seven were winners, five of stakes races.

From that first small crop of Northern Dancer foals came three champions: Viceregal – Champion Two-year-old and Horse of the Year in Canada in 1968; Dance Act – Canada's Champion Older Horse and Champion Handicap Horse in 1970, and Champion Handicap Horse again in 1971; and One For All – Champion Grass Horse in Canada in 1971. Owned and bred by John A. Bell III, one of the first US horsemen to have one of his mares bred to Northern Dancer, One For All raced mainly in the US, but won the Canadian International.

On 17 October 1968, E.P. Taylor announced that Northern Dancer would follow a route taken before and since by Canadian celebrities seeking fame and fortune: he would move to the United States. Northern Dancer's new address would be the Maryland division of Windfields Farm.

'It was a difficult decision,' said Taylor. 'He's a Canadian hero and has done well here. But in justice to his promising future, I think we must make him more accessible to the finest mares in North America.'

Although there were several large thoroughbred breeding farms in Maryland, the vast majority of North America's finest mares were roaming Kentucky's blue-grass paddocks. Kentucky mares booked to Northern Dancer still faced a 12- to 14-hour van ride. In fact, the drive from Kentucky to Oshawa is the same – 600 miles – as it is from Kentucky to Maryland. If accessibility had been the real motivation, Northern Dancer would have been sent to Kentucky. On the other hand, since Northern Dancer's two most important sons, Nijinsky and The Minstrel, were both born in Canada, perhaps he need not have moved at all. Indeed, Taylor could probably have stood him on a barge in the middle of Lake Ontario and thoroughbred breeders would still have shipped their finest mares to him.

One factor in the decision to send him to Maryland was that several years earlier Taylor had begun a training centre a few miles down the road from Chesapeake City, Maryland, a village of quaint clapboard homes on the shores of the Chesapeake River.

Taylor was convinced that training on the farm, rather than the track, would prove better for the welfare of his horses. To that end, he purchased 700 acres across the road from Mrs Richard C. du Pont's Woodstock Farm in Cecil County. It was a perfect location for a training centre. There were a number of racetracks within easy vanning distance; the quiet rolling hills and luxuriant green pastures provided ideal grazing land; and the state of Maryland offered tax incentives for raising and breeding thoroughbred horses. Taylor, of course, loved building things, so it wasn't long before the training centre had grown into one of the world's finest showcase thoroughbred farms.

Mere months prior to announcing that Northern Dancer was leaving Canada, Taylor sold his Toronto Windfields Farm, which had become hemmed in by housing developments. He did, however, keep the house and about thirty acres, which included his office and small barn for his riding horses. (The National Stud Farm would now be called Windfields.)

Northern Dancer arrived in Maryland on 3 December 1968. Three months earlier, the first of those serendipitous events that would ultimately focus international attention on Northern Dancer had taken place.

The stage was the annual Canadian Thoroughbred Horse Society Yearling Sale. The star was a big bay son of Northern Dancer, who pranced down the gravel path between the rows of grey concrete stables leading to the Woodbine sales pavilion. This supremely athletic animal was an elegant combination of power and grace, infinitely superior to the other young horses in the auction.

Already taller than most, he looked taller still because he carried his head so high. His large eyes were as soft as a deer's, yet they scanned the area warily. In the centre of his wide forehead was a patch of white in the shape of a heart. This prominent and unusual marking was an omen, for this horse had truly inherited the heart of his sire.

It was twilight at the sprawling Woodbine racetrack. Throughout the day crowds of prospective buyers had prowled the rows of stables, inspecting the 214 thoroughbred yearlings; curious onlookers had been looking at who was looking.

Taylor had decided to include the second crop of Northern Dancer offspring, along with all the other Windfields yearlings, in the annual Canadian breeders' sale, thereby turning the provincial event into an international affair. Never had so many big-time buyers been represented at a sale of Canadian thoroughbreds.

Most of the crowd had crammed into the sales pavilion. The seats formed a semi-circle around a horseshoe-shaped ring, where one by one the young horses were led back and forth in front of the audience. Above the ring the auctioneer, Laddie Dance, gavel in hand, chanted the bids, while his partner, John Finney, recounted the bloodlines of each animal. Shrewd professionals, they provoked and cajoled prospective buyers into higher and higher bids. They were dressed in tuxedos, as were the 'spotters', who hovered like hawks in search of prey, scanning their section of the theatre for the slightest sign of interest.

At the flick of a wrist or nod of a head indicating a bid, the spotter yelled, 'Yip!' and the electronic board on the wall to the right of the auctioneer's stand registered the increased stakes. While the players duelled for the animal, the rest of the audience remained still: an innocent wave to a friend and one might suddenly own a horse. When the top bid had been wrung out of the combatants, Laddie Dance slammed down the gavel with an emphatic 'Sold!' and the animal was led away. The audience could then talk and move about freely until the next horse entered the ring.

Every seat in the theatre was occupied and the walkway around the upper rim was packed with spectators anticipating the bidding duel for a certain big bay.

In the centre of the ring, the Northern Dancer colt stopped dead in his tracks. Like a statue, he stood motionless, his bright and wary eyes scanning the faces focused on him.

The bidding couldn't begin until Finney was finished with his preamble. He spoke slowly, describing the racing careers of Northern Dancer and the colt's dam, Flaming Page.

'Who will give me $60,000?' asked Laddie Dance at last, beginning with Taylor's reserve bid. If no one was willing to pay that sum, Taylor would take back the colt.

Bids bounced up from all corners of the arena, and spectators strained to see who they were coming from. Less than two minutes later Laddie Dance shouted, 'Sold for $84,000!' and slammed down the gavel.

The majestic son of Northern Dancer and Flaming Page was led out of the ring and back to his stall. Several days later he was on an aeroplane bound for Ireland – and unprecedented glory. His new owner, Charles Engelhard, named the colt after Vaslav Nijinsky.

At the time of his death in 1950, the Russian ballet star believed not only that he was a horse, but that he would be reincarnated as a horse. Eighteen years later the horse named Nijinsky arrived at Vincent O'Brien's Ballydoyle training centre, not far from Cashel, County Tipperary.

Nijinsky would be the first of many sons of Northern Dancer to make the trip to Ballydoyle. O'Brien possessed a genius with horses, particularly difficult and highly-strung ones, as the Northern Dancers often were; and he trained more Northern Dancer offspring – including Nijinsky, The Minstrel, Woodstream, El Gran Senor and Sadler's Wells – than any other trainer.

How Nijinsky ended up at Ballydoyle with Vincent O'Brien was another case of serendipity. Although Charles Engelhard had owned thoroughbreds for only nine years, he embraced the game with great enthusiasm, and on a grand scale. At the time he approached Vincent O'Brien to travel to Canada to look at a Ribot colt Windfields was offering at the September sale, Engelhard employed four trainers in England, one in the United States, one in France and another in South Africa.

O'Brien didn't like the Ribot colt, but while he was at Windfields the staff showed him the rest of the yearlings. O'Brien advised Engelhard against buying the Ribot colt, but suggested that he purchase the son of Northern Dancer and Flaming Page. Engelhard agreed, and said he would have one of his Canadian executives go to the sale.

O'Brien was anxious. 'This man of Charlie's was entirely inexperienced where the buying of horses was concerned. And so I was worried what he might do. That he'd make some slip up . . . and that I'd lose the horse.'

His other concern was Garfield Weston. Mastermind of the Weston food empire, which included Weston bakeries, the Loblaws supermarket chain, and Fortnum and Mason, Weston did bid on the colt, but eventually conceded. Charlie's man, George Scott, won the colt for his boss.

Once Nijinsky was safely in O'Brien's yard, however, the colt gave O'Brien plenty to fret about. No sooner had he arrived than he turned his nose up at O'Brien's finest Irish oats. As hungry as he must have been, Nijinsky sniffed at his feed tub each mealtime and turned away to munch on hay. After two days, O'Brien placed an urgent transatlantic call to Windfields Farm. He was told that the colt had been raised on a diet of crunch: compressed cubes of oats, bran, molasses and supplements. O'Brien asked them to ship him a supply immediately. Of course, the day the special mixture arrived Nijinsky decided to eat Irish oats.

But O'Brien's difficulties with Nijinsky had merely begun. Once he was eating, the challenge was to get him out of his stall. Most horses leave their stalls willingly. Not Nijinsky. He'd rear straight up and fight every inch of the way. Nor did he stop rearing once they got him out into the yard. He did not like to canter along with the other horses. When they eventually got him going he galloped like a seasoned show horse, but if they stopped, even for a second, he'd rear up again. Years later, when Nijinsky was celebrated as a great champion, the lads in O'Brien's Ballydoyle yard saw his ability to rear straight up as proof of his remarkable balance. At the time, however, it was a source of frustration and consternation.

Nijinsky put O'Brien in an unenviable position. Charles Engelhard was a new, potentially excellent client, and O'Brien had persuaded Engelhard both to buy this colt and to ship him to Ireland – an investment of close to $100,000. Would Charles Engelhard continue to trust O'Brien's judgement?

O'Brien wrote to Engelhard to explain the situation: 'I am somewhat concerned about Nijinsky's temperament and that he is inclined to resent getting on with his work. My best boys are riding him and we can only hope he will go the right way.'

No sooner had O'Brien informed Engelhard that Nijinsky's disposition might jeopardise the promise O'Brien had seen in the colt than Nijinsky settled into the training routine. He continued to be wilful and volatile, but once his handlers were adjusted to his restive nature, he became more co-operative. Like his sire and so many of his exceptional ancestors, he couldn't, or wouldn't, be pushed around.

Vincent O'Brien praised the talents of his resident riders, Johnny Brabston and Danny O'Sullivan, in their handling of this challenging animal: 'Nijinsky could easily have been spoiled. They had the strength to handle him and the patience not to knock him about.'

Most of the credit, however, must go to Vincent O'Brien. Son of a County Cork farmer who kept a small racing stable, young

Vincent had always been enthralled by horses. After boarding-school, he convinced his father to allow him to forsake higher education to pursue his dream of working with them. He spent a year with a trainer at Leopardstown, then returned to the family farm to groom, train and ride in point-to-point meets.

O'Brien went on to become a successful trainer of steeplechasers; he saddled three consecutive Grand National winners, his Cottage Rake won the Cheltenham Gold Cup three years in a row, and Hatton's Grace took the Cheltenham Champion Hurdle Cup in three consecutive years. In the spring of 1959, O'Brien quit, training steeplechasers to concentrate on the 'flats'.

Three years later he won the Epsom Derby with Larkspur, owned by the US ambassador to Ireland, Raymond Guest, and won the Derby again with Guest's Sir Ivor in 1968, several months before Nijinsky arrived at Ballydoyle.

Like O'Brien, E.P. Taylor saw something special in Nijinsky, and followed his career closely. The Taylors and their son, Charles, flew to Ireland for Nijinsky's first race, the Erne Stakes at The Curragh, in early July. Nijinsky won easily. After the race his exuberant rider, Irish champion jockey Liam Ward, was lavish in his praise of Nijinsky:

> You could do anything with him. He went into the stalls like a hack and came out of them and settled wherever you wanted to put him. You could ride him on a silver thread . . . He just did everything. You could sit and wait all day because he had this terrific speed.
>
> He was such a good ride that you could drop him in behind horses anywhere at all, just whenever you felt like it. Pull him out and say 'Go' and that was it. He went into another gear immediately . . . it was just a matter of whenever you wanted to win on him, that was it.

Nijinsky went to the post five times as a two-year-old and barely had to move beyond a canter to win all five races, four in Ireland and the Dewhurst Stakes at England's Newmarket course. The ease with which he won the Dewhurst – considered a preview of the horses likely to contest the following year's classic races – inspired some controversy over Nijinsky's ability.

Timeform: Racehorses of 1969 praised Nijinsky: 'Only a horse right out of the top drawer could have treated his opponents in such an off-hand manner . . . a horse of the highest class. Everything about him is impressive . . . Small wonder he is looked upon as an exciting prospect for the Classics.'

Other experts, however, saw Nijinsky's breeding as suspect. Knowing that Northern Dancer had not won the Belmont, they were convinced that his son would not be able to handle the mile-and-a-half distance of the Derby.

As a serious contender for the classic races, Nijinsky would require different training and conditioning from the other horses in O'Brien's yard. Nijinsky, however, had ideas of his own, and O'Brien was faced with the dilemma of maintaining a schedule that would suit the rest of the horses while accommodating the temperamental and wilful colt.

As soon as the first lot of horses was readied for their morning work, Nijinsky would start to fret. He didn't like being left behind in his stall. Eventually O'Brien conceived a plan that suited Nijinsky's disposition: each morning the crew brought him out with the others and let him warm up with them. When the first lot went off to gallop, Nijinsky was ridden over to a large barn where, with another horse, he walked around until it was time for him to be worked.

Vincent O'Brien's insight into Nijinsky's nature was recorded in *Nijinsky: Triple Crown Winner* by Richard Baerlein:

> Most good horses take it easy at home . . . Sir Ivor for instance just worked with whatever horse he was working with. No matter how bad the latter was, Sir Ivor would just head him, and that was that, no more.
>
> Nijinsky, once he hit the front, pricked his ears and went on from there, galloping away from the other horses, which was quite remarkable and most unusual . . . He didn't require a lot of work . . . He was active all the time, once he went out to exercise in the morning. He was exercising himself all the time. He wasn't just ambling about, but always alert and using himself. Therefore he was a horse that was at his best when lightly trained.

Nijinsky made his debut as a three-year-old at The Curragh in the Gladness Stakes. With Liam Ward in the saddle, he cruised to another easy victory. He now had six wins in six starts. His next scheduled appearance was at Newmarket for the first of the British Triple Crown races, the Two Thousand Guineas.

The bookmakers were among those who saw Nijinsky's breeding as suspect, and undervalued his chances in the early betting. It was rumoured that they would lose close to $1 million if the colt won. The ever vigilant O'Brien hired a private detective to complement Newmarket's security force and guard Nijinsky around the clock.

Liam Ward would continue to ride Nijinsky in Ireland, but his jockey for the Two Thousand Guineas and the other English races was Lester Piggott. Nijinsky won the race easily by two and a half lengths. Since there was a month to go before the Derby, he returned to Ballydoyle.

Five days prior to the Derby Nijinsky was flown back to England. But instead of joining the other Derby horses training at Epsom, he was sequestered at Sandown Park. A short van ride to Epsom, Sandown offered a peaceful environment with less risk of sabotage, and was out of the media spotlight. The day before the race Nijinsky was driven to Epsom to acclimatise him to the course.

Everything was going brilliantly, when disaster struck: upon returning to the stables after his tour of the course, Nijinsky broke out into a sweat and started pawing the ground, showing all the signs of colic, including severe abdominal pain. Horses have small stomachs (thus limited digestive surface) and extremely long intestinal tracts. Colic can be fatal for them. They are unable to vomit or belch, and food or foreign matter can be trapped in the puckers of the large intestine. Generally a drug is given to relax the intestinal walls, which are in spasm, and allow the painful gas to escape. However, the rules of racing dictated that no drugs be given a horse 24 hours before the race. The O'Brien team resorted to an old remedy employed prior to the advent of pharmaceutical companies. They gathered fresh grass and mixed it with bicarbonate of soda and bran. Their offering – and, no doubt, their prayers – worked: within a couple of hours Nijinsky was back to normal.

The course of the Derby, one and a half miles of twists, turns, hills and dales, is the most demanding in the world. It requires great stamina, agility, speed, and courage of its contestants.

The field of 11 on Derby Day, 3 June 1970, included Gyr, the giant chestnut from France. His trainer, Etienne Pollet, was so convinced Gyr would not only win the Derby but sweep the three-year-old Classics that he had postponed his retirement for a year in order to run him. Other extremely good horses in the race were Approval, Meadowville and the unbeaten Stintino.

In the paddock before the race Nijinsky was sweating and appeared anxious; however, once in his starting stall he calmed down. Nijinsky broke well and Lester Piggott settled him into the centre of the pack. There they coasted around the first slight turn to the left and the sharper right turn.

It was about a 150-foot climb to the top of the hill that was the halfway mark, and Piggott seemed in little hurry to make a move.

The 11 horses galloped around the level curve to the left and down the hill to Tattenham Corner. Still no action from Nijinsky. At the Corner, some three and a half furlongs from home, several of his running mates began vying for position. With two furlongs to go, Gyr grabbed the lead.

Suddenly Nijinsky – his ears perked, his eyes focused beyond the horizon – began to accelerate. Ordinary horses have four gaits, but Nijinsky had a fifth, magical gait that grew longer and longer each time his hooves brushed the soft turf. His entire being, a powerful symphony of perfect rhythm and harmony, transcended the limits of his earthbound companions.

'My father had been to "the Guineas" and returned to England to watch Nijinsky run in the Derby,' recalled Charles Taylor. 'In a rare act of courtesy from owner to breeder, Charlie Engelhard invited my father to join him in leading Nijinsky into the winner's circle. It was a very memorable scene.'

It was nearly eighteen years since Taylor had purchased the best mare at the Newmarket sale and held firm in his resolve to have Lady Angela bred back to Nearco. To be standing in Epsom's winner's circle with Nijinsky, born of his commitment to raise classic winners in Canada, was the fulfilment of a dream beyond even Taylor's fertile imagination.

Nijinsky's next race was the Irish Derby, and again he triumphed – by three lengths, over a boggy course. His victory made him only the second horse to win both the Irish and the English Derbys. Nijinsky was, however, becoming increasingly anxious, and prior to the race he had fretted himself into a lather.

'Nijinsky sweated up quite a bit before the race,' recalled his jockey, Liam Ward. 'He got on his toes a lot and I am sure he had run one race by the time we got to the stalls. From the moment he jumped out, however, I was never in any doubt that I was going to win. I was never out of half-speed all the way on him. He did everything I asked him to do that day.'

Nijinsky had a month back at Ballydoyle to restore his energy and prepare for his next race, the King George VI and Queen Elizabeth Stakes, on 25 July at Ascot. He was the lone three-year-old among the finest older horses in the world, including the previous year's Derby winner, Blakeney; Crepellana, the previous year's French Oaks winner; Italian Derby winner, Hogarth; and Coronation winner, Caliban. Because of the calibre of the field and the ease and brilliance with which Nijinsky ran the mile-and-a-half contest, this race was considered his most impressive performance.

'Probably Nijinsky's best race ever,' enthused his jockey, Lester Piggott, 'because he was up against good older horses and he still won in a canter . . . I have never been more impressed with a horse.'

Nijinsky was so brilliant, so vastly superior to all other horses, that simply watching him run, witnessing his magical acceleration, became a treasured memory of many throughout the British Isles. To have been at the Guineas, or the Derby, or any of Nijinsky's races, was an experience to boast of and to cherish.

Northern Dancer was well on his way to establishing himself as a powerful young stallion in North America, but it was Nijinsky that turned Northern Dancer into an international celebrity. Had Nijinsky not been so extraordinary, it is unlikely that Northern Dancer's domination would have spread world-wide and affected thoroughbred racing and breeding so profoundly. Yet, at the time, the international racing community turned their heads only briefly in the direction of Nijinsky's sire, then went back to discounting Northern Dancer as a stallion of importance. They were, however, prepared to wager on Nijinsky as a prospective stallion.

Not surprisingly, the British wanted to keep Nijinsky in England, and were prepared to go as high as $3 million. An Irish group countered with $4 million. However, on 14 August 1970, it was announced that Nijinsky had been syndicated for a world record $5.4 million, and would be standing in Kentucky at Claiborne Farm.

North American syndications in the 1970s were divided into 32 shares; British syndications comprised 40 to 43 shares. Each share entitled the owner to one breeding right, the opportunity to send one mare each year to the syndicated stallion.

Each of the 32 shares in Nijinsky was valued at $170,000. Charles Engelhard kept ten shares for himself and offered Taylor two shares. Taylor willingly paid the $340,000 for a small interest in the colt he had sold for $84,000 two years earlier.

A week after Nijinsky returned to Ballydoyle from Ascot he broke out in a severe case of ringworm, a fungus that grows rapidly over the hide. The condition creates an inflammation of the skin and hair follicles, resulting in hair loss in the affected areas. The ringworm spread around Nijinsky's girth and the area behind the withers where the saddle sits. Since it was impossible to put a saddle on his tender back, the grooms at Ballydoyle walked Nijinsky by hand, around and around the yard to exercise him.

L'Arc de Triomphe, the next and final race on Nijinsky's schedule, was still two months away, so there was no great cause for alarm. Nijinsky was, after all, extremely fit and strong, which would help expedite his recovery.

In the meantime, Nijinsky continued to be the main topic of British racing. The general consensus, from local pubs to private clubs, was that it was highly improbable that any of them would see a horse of Nijinsky's class ever again.

It wasn't long before the British racing press began echoing these sentiments, and were clamouring for an encore. They wanted Nijinsky to run in the St Leger, the final race in the British Triple Crown. No horse had won all three races – the Guineas, the Derby, and the St Leger – since Bahram, in 1935.

Eventually Nijinsky's itinerary was changed to include the St Leger. Run over the pear-shaped Doncaster course in Yorkshire, the race is 14 furlongs 127 yards – nearly two miles.

On 12 September 1970, Nijinsky won the St Leger – and the British Triple Crown. Although he appeared to run this, his eleventh race, with accustomed ease, it would be his last victory.

The nearly two-mile test and, no doubt, the effect of the ringworm on his system had taken a toll: O'Brien, who was unusual among trainers at the time in that he weighed his horses before and after every race, found that Nijinsky had lost 30 pounds in the St Leger.

Lester Piggott's opinion of his mount for his fifth St Leger victory was that 'the Leger was too far for him. He had been off the track for quite some time and he had this skin disease. Actually, he had a very easy race, but the distance, I think, took that much more out of him than it had done in any previous race.'

Three weeks later Nijinsky was at Longchamps in the Bois de Boulogne, a few miles from the centre of Paris, for the Prix de l'Arc de Triomphe. The mile-and-a-half French classic is one of the world's premier thoroughbred races. Run in early autumn, for three-year-olds and up, the Arc is said to 'set the seal' on the post-racing career of a horse.

When Nijinsky arrived in the walking ring the area turned into a mob scene. Hordes of photographers and reporters pressed in on the already distressed horse; a television crew member inadvertently shoved a microphone into Nijinsky's nostril; the enormous crowd outside the ring clapped and shouted. By the time Nijinsky walked on to the course, he was coated in a white lather. His fragile nerves were shot.

Piggott kept Nijinsky well back in the early stages of the race. Then, somehow, he was in the middle of the field, with no running room. Hemmed in by the previous year's Epsom Derby winner, Blakeney, he had run into a wall of horses.

Coming down to the wire, Piggott was forced to take Nijinsky out and around the other horses to gain running room. Going wide consumed precious time and strides in the last seconds, and the French horse, Sassafras, was out in front. Piggott crouched low, almost lying on Nijinsky's neck. With only 50 yards to go, the horses were running in unison, with Nijinsky a fraction ahead of Sassafras. Recognising that Nijinsky's once magical acceleration was no longer there, Piggott cracked him with the whip to keep him going. Nijinsky had never been hit before, and he tried to duck the punishment at the very moment the horses crossed the wire. In a photo finish Sassafras won by a nostril, and a tired Nijinsky was led back to his stall.

If he had won the Arc, it would have been his final race; however, Engelhard and O'Brien decided to run him one more time, in the Championship Stakes, two weeks later at Newmarket. 'I felt I owed it to the horse to give him the chance to make his last appearance a winning one,' explained Vincent O'Brien.

The largest crowd in the history of Newmarket turned out to cheer Nijinsky. He appeared to be in peak condition, but as the applause and shouts of encouragement followed him from the walking ring to the course, his nerves frayed. He simply could no longer take the pressure.

Nijinsky ran smoothly right up behind the leaders, but when it came to that last furlong drive, the magic was gone and he finished second again to an inferior animal.

Charles Engelhard reflected the sentiments of Nijinsky's admirers in an interview with Gerald Strine of the *Washington Post*: 'Nijinsky was a great one. I think, though, that to ask your horse, in a single year, to win over a variety of distances, over different courses, and under the different conditions was unfair.

'I think that the number and type of races that this horse was asked to win is perhaps more than one can normally ask any animal. This is one of the reasons that in my opinion, we as humans let him down.'

Only months later, in March 1971, Charles Engelhard died at the age of 54.

When Nijinsky arrived at Claiborne Farm, he would be known as Nijinsky II, since there was already a Nijinsky standing at stud in the United States – neither a great racehorse nor a stallion of any importance. The Jockey Clubs in Great Britain and North America maintain separate registries; thus the existence of the vastly inferior US Nijinsky necessitated a name change for the son of Northern Dancer to Nijinsky II.

Nijinsky II, like his father, became an outstanding sire of winners and champions. In 1982, his son Golden Fleece won the Epsom Derby. In 1986, his son Ferdinand won the Kentucky Derby. A month later another son, Shahrastani, won the Epsom Derby. His son Seattle Dancer was the highest-priced thoroughbred yearling sold at public auction, for $13.2 million. Many of his sons became sires of champions, and his daughters dams of champions.

Yet Nijinsky will always be remembered as quite possibly the most magnificent and exciting racehorse of all time. He was truly special, and witnessing him glide into that magical fifth gait of his is forever etched in the memory of all who saw him run. To be associated with him was to touch the stars. And so it was that a group of Englishmen and Irishmen set out in search of another Nijinsky and, in the process, stumbled upon a veritable wellspring of extraordinary horses: daughters and sons of Northern Dancer.

The Extraordinary
Nature of the Beasts

The time was fast approaching when people would spend any amount, no matter how outrageous, to possess one of Northern Dancer's offspring. And, sooner or later, thieves were bound to realise that anything that valuable was worth kidnapping.

At 4 p.m., on 25 June 1977, a member of the Claiborne Farm staff counted nine brood mares grazing lazily in the south field adjacent to Barn 4. Two and a half hours later the night watchman counted eight. Fanfreluche, a daughter of Northern Dancer from the same foal crop as Nijinsky, and owned by Canadian Jean-Louis Lévesque, was missing.

The first clues in what proved to be a mystery worthy of Dick Francis were a panel of wire fence that was cut, then roughly reattached; a plastic garbage bag found in the bushes nearby, half-filled with sweet alfalfa hay; and a set of hoofprints leading from the fence to the driveway. Later, a neighbour told police that on each of the three days preceding Fanfreluche's disappearance he had seen the same silver-coloured Ford parked on the side of the road, not far from Claiborne's south field. Another reported seeing a green pick-up truck hauling a two-horse trailer near Claiborne at 4.40 p.m. on the day of the theft.

The FBI and the local police pieced together a scenario. Presumably the thieves had been watching the farm for at least three days and had enticed the mares with the alfalfa to that particular spot along the fence. On the day of the theft, police and Claiborne staff reasoned, the thieves again lured the brood mares over, singled out Fanfreluche, and cut through the wire fence. Once they had Fanfreluche they hastily repaired the fence before the other mares got loose, loaded Fanfreluche on the trailer, and sped off.

From each of the three homes in the immediate vicinity, including owner Seth Hancock's Victorian-style mansion, the view of that section of the paddock was completely obstructed – by a large oak on one side and a sugar maple on the other.

Nonetheless, a theft on a Saturday afternoon, only a few hundred yards from Hancock's home, smacked of 'insider information'. Whether the thieves knew that Hancock was out golfing that day was unclear, but they were certainly experienced with horses. Fanfreluche had her sire's wilful temperament: getting her to leave the herd and walk up the ramp into the narrow trailer would have been no mean feat. As Lévesque's son Pierre put it: 'Whoever stole Fanfreluche didn't just pick any old mare out of that paddock. They had to be after Fanfreluche. She's got a really bad temper, you see. She hates people. She'd give them an awful fight . . . We're speculating, and so are the police, that these people had to have inside information because Fanfreluche would have given them so much trouble.'

Heightening the concern of all involved was the fact that Fanfreluche was more than two months pregnant, in foal to Secretariat. Moreover, Fanfreluche was, according to Claiborne's veterinarian, 'a habitual aborter' and was on special medication to maintain her pregnancy: without the drug there was a 90 per cent chance that she would miscarry. Not only was Fanfreluche's life at serious risk, but so was that of her unborn foal.

Why Fanfreluche? Small, compact and volatile, she was very much like her sire, and had been an outstanding racehorse. In 1970, while Nijinsky was being celebrated in Great Britain, Fanfreluche was named Canadian Horse of the Year and Champion Three-year-old Filly in the United States and Canada.

Trainer J. 'Yonnie' Starr recalled her to *Toronto Star* columnist Milt Dunnell: 'When I saw Fanfreluche as a yearling I noticed she was small but well-made and there was something about her I liked. Then after I worked her a few times I started to think we had something special.

'How can you forget that day in Winnipeg when the Queen was there? The track was as bad as I ever have seen. Yet I had not thought of taking her out of the race [Manitoba Derby] because I knew she would run over it easily.'

She also won the Alabama Stakes (Saratoga), the Quebec Derby, set a new track record in the Benson and Hedges International, and was second in the Queen's Plate and the Spinster Stakes (Keeneland). As a three-year-old Fanfreluche was sent to the post 15 times, and only once was she out of the money.

But Fanfreluche's racing days were long past. She was retired in the autumn of 1970 and had become a brood mare. There was, of course, a good chance that Fanfreluche possessed an abundance of Northern Dancer's 'super-genes'. She had produced four foals, three of which were champions: L'Enjoleur, winner of the Laurel Futurity and Queen's Plate, and two-time Canadian Horse of the Year; La Voyageuse, Champion Three-year-old Filly in Canada, Champion Older Mare in Canada, and Champion Sprinter in Canada; and Médaille d'Or, Champion Two-year-old Colt in Canada, and her first foal by Secretariat.

Although she was valued at more than half a million dollars, Fanfreluche was nowhere near the most highly prized animal at Claiborne. The farm was home to 325 of the world's finest blue-blood mares. There was also a herd of several hundred impeccably bred weanlings and yearlings with great racing potential. Only a few hundred yards from where Fanfreluche was stolen, 24 of the world's most prominent stallions, including Nijinsky II, Buckpasser, Round Table and Secretariat, roamed their paddocks.

So why Fanfreluche? Some immediately suspected extortion, and others wondered whether it was significant that the theft of Fanfreluche coincided, almost to the minute, with that year's running of the Queen's Plate.

The theft, like that of Shergar several years later, might have been politically motivated. Not only did Lévesque have a horse, Giboulée, running in the race, he had been threatened by terrorists the year Fanfreluche had run in the Queen's Plate.

Born in the village of Nouvelle, in the Gaspé region of Quebec, the young Jean-Louis Lévesque was fired from his job as a bank teller. The manager told him he would never make it in the banking business. Years later, the charming and shrewd Jean-Louis was wealthy enough to buy the bank. Chairman of the board of the brokerage firm Lévesque, Beaubien Inc., the successful and prominent businessman had been a target of Québécois separatist terrorists because he was a proponent of a united Canada. (Lévesque even included a maple leaf on the front of his racing silks.)

On the eve of the 1970 Queen's Plate, Lévesque's Montreal home was bombed by separatist terrorists, outraged that he would run Fanfreluche in a race honouring the British monarchy.

Seven years later, when Fanfreluche was kidnapped, neither terrorists nor extortionists were heard from. Long days rolled into longer weeks. There were no ransom demands, no notes, no calls despite a $25,000 reward for information leading to identification of the thieves. The eerie silence could mean only one thing: Fanfreluche was dead. Everyone except Jean-Louis Lévesque gave up hope of seeing her alive.

Early in December, five and a half months after being stolen, Fanfreluche was found on a tumbledown farm near Tompkinsville, Kentucky, 130 miles south-west of Lexington. She had been named Brandy by her new family, and was being used as a riding horse. Other than signs of rope burns above her hooves and a long, shaggy winter coat, Fanfreluche was in good shape, and still in foal.

'They'd been feeding her cracked corn and something like mule feed,' Seth Hancock reported. 'She stayed in good flesh. She was getting good hay down there. They had a big bale of alfalfa sitting there.'

The thieves must have pulled over on a side road, taken Fanfreluche off the trailer, then driven off, leaving the disorientated mare to fend for herself in the backwoods of Kentucky.

The Tompkinsville farmer usually had a couple of ponies or saddle horses, so when a neighbour saw Fanfreluche trotting down the road all on her own, he put a rope on her and led her to the farmer, assuming she belonged to him. She didn't, of course, but the farmer thought she might make a decent riding horse for his wife if no one claimed her. He reported finding the mare to the local sheriff, but no one made the connection to Fanfreluche.

Throughout the summer and autumn, Fanfreluche – alias Brandy – lived out of doors with several riding horses in a small lot enclosed by a single strand of electric wire. When winter came she spent the nights in a tiny makeshift stall in the corner of a storage shed.

The farmer's wife apparently wasn't fond of riding 'Brandy' as she found her stubborn and mean tempered. That she rode her at all speaks highly, however, of the wife's equestrian abilities. With the exception of exercise riders, the only other person to ride Fanfreluche was champion jockey Ron Turcotte. The farmer's wife had planned to ride Brandy at the head of a local parade, the day after it was discovered that Brandy was Fanfreluche. A week earlier a horse trader had offered the farm couple $200 for her; he wanted to put her in a riding-horse auction in Nashville, Tennessee. For a time they were tempted to sell, but in the end they declined; they had grown fond of Brandy, despite her disposition.

'When I was walking her into the van,' said Hancock, 'these two old women were standing there crying, "Oh, there goes Brandy".'

Several hours later, Brandy was back to being Fanfreluche at Claiborne's exclusive 3,200-acre horse nursery. Although the veterinarians had been certain she would miscarry without monthly injections of the progesterone depodeprovera, the following February she gave birth to a foal. He was named Sain et Sauf – 'safe and sound'.

The female side of the Northern Dancer bloodline has often been overshadowed, by megamillion-dollar stallion syndications and the promotion of the male line. Yet many Northern Dancer fillies were like their sire not only physically but also in temperament.

The female line has produced racehorses that are, in some instances, vastly superior to their male counterparts: granddaughters Three Troikas (Arc de Triomphe winner and Horse of the Year in France) and Dance Smartly (Canadian Triple Crown winner and Horse of the Year) are but two examples.

Many were also dams of champions and exceptional racehorses. In 1993, Japan's Champion Two-year-old, Narita Brian, and Champion Three-year-old and Horse of the Year, Biwa Hayahide, were both out of the mare Pacificus, a Windfields-bred-and-born daughter of Northern Dancer.

Fanfreluche was a true Northern Dancer, both in size and in disposition. She was tough, often ornery, frequently volatile. And as with so many Northern Dancers, she was extremely difficult to handle, yet she ran like a demon.

The trauma of being stolen from the rest of the herd, abandoned on a sideroad, and kept in a small pen might well have unhinged a highly-strung thoroughbred like Fanfreluche. Yet she not only survived the ordeal, she didn't miscarry – a tribute, no doubt, to her toughness.

A week after Fanfreluche was kidnapped, the toughness of the

Northern Dancers was brought to world attention. The horse was The Minstrel, and the stage was the Epsom Derby.

In 1970, when Nijinsky won the Derby, attention was focused briefly on Northern Dancer, but only briefly, since Nijinsky did not resemble his sire. The perception at the time in Great Britain and Europe was that North American horses were bred solely for speed, and they lacked the stamina for the longer-distance races. Northern Dancer's failure to win the Belmont was seen as evidence of this fundamental weakness. Nijinsky must have been a fluke.

Seven years later, when The Minstrel became Northern Dancer's second son to win the Derby, attention again turned to Northern Dancer. This time he was taken more seriously. It wouldn't be long before Northern Dancer's offspring were more valuable than gold, and all because of the Epsom Derby.

To walk into the winner's circle leading the Derby champion is the ultimate dream of thoroughbred owners the world over. In the sport of kings and queens, the Epsom Derby not only bestows tremendous prestige, but also assures the owners a place in history. The winning horse will be standing on the same ground as its celebrated ancestors. If you listen closely, you can almost hear the hoofbeats of the great legends galloping across the turf on their way to Epsom's winner's circle: Hyperion, Sir Ivor, Mill Reef, Sea Bird II, Shergar, Nijinsky. Their sweat is in the soil, their breath in the air.

For more than 200 years, the Derby has been the Holy Grail of thoroughbred racing, and has set the standard for the breed. It is no ordinary horse race. The course at Epsom is ideal: lush turf, well drained by the chalk beneath the surface. The mile-and-a-half Derby begins with an uphill climb, followed by a steep descent around the tight Tattenham Corner. The course then straightens and flattens until the final furlong, where the ground rises again. Each stage of the race offers its unique challenges. Many good horses have come unstuck negotiating Tattenham Corner, especially big horses the size of Nijinsky; and the final uphill ascent to the finish is surely the supreme test of courage, stamina and the will to win.

By the time the first Derby was run at Epsom in 1780, horse racing over the downs had already been conducted for at least a century. The immortal Eclipse ran – and won – his first race, four one-mile heats, over this very ground on 3 May 1769.

The mineral springs at Epsom were discovered in 1618 by a

farmer when he noticed his cows refused to drink from a particular puddle on their grazing land. It was determined that the water bubbling up from underground springs contained restorative and laxative properties, and before long the area became a spa. Local entrepreneurs offered horse racing as an added enticement to visitors.

The downs provided soft, natural turf, which, according to one scribe, 'was covered with grass finer than Persian carpets and perfumed with wild thyme and juniper'. Yet, for most of the 1700s, the waters, gaming houses and parties of Epsom attracted far more attention than the horse races.

The inspiration for the Derby came in the summer of 1779, when the twelfth Earl of Derby was hosting a party near Epsom at The Oaks, a converted inn that had belonged to his uncle, General Burgoyne. Derby's filly, Bridget, had just won the inaugural Oaks – a race restricted to three-year-old fillies – which Derby and his friends had devised at a party at the inn the previous year, hence the name, the Oaks.

While celebrating the success of the Oaks, Derby and his friends decided to create a separate race to include both three-year-old fillies and colts the following year. Once the concept was agreed upon, they needed a name. But for a flip of a coin, the world's most distinguished horse race might have been called the Epsom Bunbury. Sir Charles Bunbury a respected member of England's racing fraternity may have lost the toss, but he won the first Derby with his colt Diomed.

By the early 1800s, the Derby had become recognised as England's most prestigious and best-attended horse-racing event. Its early status was due largely to its location: a mere 15 miles south-west of London, and increasingly accessible as Britain's railway system grew. The Derby had become so popular by the mid-nineteenth century that the British Parliament called a recess on Derby Day. Lord Palmerston described the Derby as 'our Olympic Games'.

The magnificent Nijinsky looked as if he might just have galloped down from Mount Olympus, but The Minstrel was, except for his colour, a duplicate of Northern Dancer. He had enormous heart, courage, determination and stamina, and he possessed Northern Dancer's toughness. Vincent O'Brien considered The Minstrel one of the toughest horses he ever worked with.

Initially, it was The Minstrel's resemblance to Northern Dancer that gave Vincent O'Brien serious doubts about buying the colt at the 1975 Keeneland sale – he was concerned about his size. Five years earlier he had passed up a yearling son of Northern Dancer out of the mare Goofed at the Newmarket yearling sale. The colt was almost a double of Northern Dancer: he was the same colour; the white blaze down the centre of his face was almost identical; and, like his sire, he was small.

That horse was named Lyphard, and he proved a Group I (the classification given the most important races) winner in France. Lyphard stood his first season as a stallion in 1973, and soon would become renowned as a dynamic sire of great champions. When O'Brien considered The Minstrel, no doubt he thought of Lyphard.

Vincent O'Brien went to the Keeneland sales that muggy July in 1975 specifically to buy The Minstrel. O'Brien's travelling companions included his new business partners, Robert Sangster and John Magnier. They had their sights set on The Minstrel simply because he was a three-quarter brother to Nijinsky. A son of Northern Dancer, his dam was Fleur, a daughter of Nijinsky's dam, Flaming Page, moreover, he had been bred and born on the same farm as his sire and Nijinsky. The colt looked good on paper, but in the days before the sale O'Brien and his team returned again and again to the Windfields stable area to inspect and reinspect the animal.

'I was definitely concerned about his height,' O'Brien recalled. 'I remember going back to his box more than once to see if I could make myself feel any easier about it.'

The colt was a deep golden chestnut with a wide white blaze the entire length of his face. If Vincent O'Brien didn't already have misgivings about buying the colt because of his size, this young son of Northern Dancer had white stockings running from his hooves up his slender cannon bones almost to his knees, on all four legs.

There is a superstition among horse buyers that goes like this: One white sock: buy the horse; two white socks: try the horse; three white socks: doubt the horse; four white socks: go without the horse. (Both Northern Dancer and Nijinsky had three white socks.) There is no scientific evidence to support this superstition, just a theory that areas of lighter pigmentation may be more susceptible to skin afflictions.

Over the centuries all sorts of theories about horses' markings have been proposed. In 1669, G.B. Trutta advised: 'The horse with a white mark on his right foot is to be avoided, for horses thus marked are disastrous in their performance. [Nijinsky was so marked.] If all four feet are white and the horse also has white in his face, he will be of gentle disposition, but of scant success in action.' While Trutta's theories may now seem quaint, they were probably based on as much fact as our 'four white socks: go without the horse' superstition.

After great deliberation, Vincent O'Brien defied the superstition, overcame his misgivings about the animal's size, and paid $200,000 – top dollar at the time – to buy the colt on behalf of his new partnership.

Back in Ireland, as O'Brien began working with the colt, he discovered that The Minstrel's nature was as different from Nijinsky's as his physique. Whereas Nijinsky was volatile, difficult and acutely sensitive, The Minstrel was willing, eager and thoroughly rugged. The characteristics they had in common were courage and an abundance of heart.

The Minstrel enthusiastically took to training over the Ballydoyle gallops. Always eager to get out and run, he was absolutely tenacious, determined to finish at the head of the pack. Unlike Nijinsky, he didn't turn his nose up at O'Brien's Irish oats; he didn't rear and refuse to come out of his stall; he didn't throw temper tantrums. He simply worked and worked.

Generally O'Brien started the two-year-old classic hopefuls in July, but he held The Minstrel back until September 8, when the eager colt won the Moy Stakes at The Curragh by five lengths. Although he wasn't challenged by any horse in the field, The Minstrel set a new track record. Two weeks later he won the Larkspur Stakes at Leopardstown.

After passing those two Irish tests, he was considered ready for the Dewhurst Stakes at Newmarket, the race Nijinsky had run and won easily seven years earlier. The Minstrel galloped to a decisive four-length victory in this most important two-year-old competition, yet most of the racing crowd remained unimpressed with him. They had been hoping to see, and thrill to, another Nijinsky.

Most great thoroughbreds race only to the end of their three-year-old year, and thus appear only briefly before the racing public. So it was natural for people to want to re-experience the magic of Nijinsky through his Canadian brother.

Time and again, The Minstrel would be compared with Nijinsky, and time and again he would be found lacking. No matter what he did, how fast he ran, how hard he tried, there was always an element of disappointment: he just wasn't Nijinsky. The Minstrel was also stigmatised as Northern Dancer had been: he was simply too small to be great.

Later Vincent O'Brien would comment: 'This Northern Dancer breed was something new in the racehorse world. They didn't have to be big to be good.'

While Northern Dancer was proving to North Americans that bigger wasn't necessarily better, The Minstrel was about to make the same point on the other side of the Atlantic. The first race on The Minstrel's three-year-old agenda was the Two Thousand Guineas Trial at Ascot, where his mettle and stamina would surely be put to the test. The ground was so boggy that the organisers were unable to get the starting gate through the mire; instead they had the horses line up and gallop off at the drop of the flag. The Minstrel slogged through the unforgiving turf and emerged, as was his wont, at the head of the pack.

The race should not have taken place over such a course. Nearly all the other horses in the field never won a race thereafter; the dreadful conditions sapped either their energy or their heart or both.

The Minstrel's Herculean effort in the Guineas trial made him the betting favourite at Newmarket for the English Two Thousand Guineas. Considering the toll the trial must have taken, a poor post position, and a slow start, it wasn't surprising he didn't win. Remarkably, The Minstrel finished third, only two lengths behind the winner.

His next race was the Irish Two Thousand Guineas at The Curragh, two weeks later. Although impeded by English Guineas winner Nebbiolo at one point, The Minstrel rallied in a valiant effort to overtake the leader. Another stride and he would have caught him. But he came in second, a short head off the winner, Pampapaul.

The question now was whether he should be run in the Epsom Derby two weeks later. He certainly had the heart and desire to win, but would he have the stamina for this most demanding race? In the eight weeks since he had ploughed through the bog at Ascot he had run three gruelling races. O'Brien thought they should bypass the Derby but The Minstrel's English jockey, Lester Piggott, convinced him that The Minstrel should run.

Even with only an average-sized crowd The Minstrel tended to get upset and break out into a sweat before a race. Given the lengthy Derby post-parade and the energy of the 300,000 Derby fans, Vincent O'Brien inserted cotton-wool into the colt's sensitive ears. After The Minstrel walked to the start, O'Brien's assistant trainer removed the cotton-wool.

Two furlongs from the finish The Minstrel was three lengths back of the leader, Hot Grove, when Piggott reached back and gave him such a crack on his quarters that the sound of the whip could be heard in the stands. Piggott continued pounding The Minstrel as if their very lives depended on being first across the wire. Such punishment would have completely unhinged Nijinsky; other horses simply would have caved in; but The Minstrel just kept charging harder and harder up the incline. In the dying seconds of the race The Minstrel made up the three lengths and a bit more, plunging past the most famous of finish posts half a length ahead of Hot Grove. The favoured French horse, Blushing Groom, was third, five lengths back.

The improbable had happened: The Minstrel, the little Canadian chestnut colt with four white socks, who could never live up to Nijinsky, had won the most important race in the world.

It wasn't a glamorous victory; he certainly didn't possess Nijinsky's magical fifth gait. The Minstrel won on sheer guts and determination, some inner drive that compelled him, from the time he entered training, to be at the head of the pack. He surely was the incarnation of his sire.

Now there could be no doubt about the stamina of this North American thoroughbred. Maybe, like Nijinsky, he was a fluke. Or perhaps these Canadian horses were different. One thing was certain: in seven years, two Canadian horses by the same Canadian stallion had won the race that defines the thoroughbred. It was time to take a closer look at the source of these remarkable animals.

The Minstrel was a harbinger of things to come; there would be many more direct descendants of Northern Dancer in the revered winner's circle. The thoroughbred was about to be recreated – and in the image of Northern Dancer.

Many British turf experts speculated that the Derby might be The Minstrel's final race. Given the other demanding races he had run, how could the colt have any reserves left?

The Minstrel returned to Ballydoyle and dug into his feed tub. Like a fit young prize-fighter, he rebounded, ready to fight his way to the top.

Three and a half weeks after the Derby he was back in the starting stalls at The Curragh for the Irish Derby. He won the race by a length and a half, despite a claim of foul against his jockey and a stewards' inquiry for possible interference in the final furlong. He was now the betting favourite for the King George VI and Queen Elizabeth Diamond Stakes at Ascot on 23 July. It would be his sixth race in 16 weeks, and he was up against a strong field, most of them a year older than he. Yet his courage and determination never waned. He won once again, by the narrowest of margins. Although scheduled to run against Alleged – also trained by O'Brien – in the Arc de Triomphe, The Minstrel was retired.

E.P. Taylor, now 76, had been following The Minstrel closely. He was convinced that the colt was the 'heir apparent' to Northern Dancer. First he offered to buy The Minstrel back – for ten times the $200,000 he had received for the horse two years earlier! He wanted to bring The Minstrel back to North America to stand at stud at Windfields.

Because of an outbreak of the virus contagious equine metritis in Great Britain and France, the US Department of Agriculture was on the verge of imposing a ban on horses shipping from those countries. Taylor had to work fast. Several days after the King George VI and Queen Elizabeth it was announced that The Minstrel had been syndicated for $9 million. Taylor held a $4.5 million half interest, and The Minstrel was flown immediately to the United States. Taylor went to Saratoga to see if he could interest his friends in buying shares in the horse.

'He was sold out in an hour or two,' recalled Charles Taylor, 'and Dad had to ask Sangster to free up two more shares to meet the demand.'

Northern Dancer was not particularly pleased to see his son: when The Minstrel arrived in Maryland Northern Dancer was visibly angry and upset. Perhaps he sensed that the young stallion threatened his supremacy.

In the fall of 1977 The Minstrel was voted Horse of the Year in both England and Ireland. He may, however, be better remembered as the son of Northern Dancer that catapulted the thoroughbred industry into a buying frenzy never experienced before or since.

For a while, it appeared that The Minstrel would become Northern Dancer's 'heir apparent'. He may have stood at stud in North America, but his offspring seemed predisposed to European turf courses. He sired 48 stakes winners, including French champion L'Emigrant, English champion Bakaroff; Irish champion Minstrella; and German champion Shicklah. From 1980 to 1984, daughters of The Minstrel fetched top dollar at Saratoga.

Unfortunately The Minstrel had to be put down on 3 September 1990, at a veterinary hospital near Lexington, Kentucky, following complications from severe laminitis, caused by toxic enteritis (inflammation of the intestines). He was 16.

The Minstrel, like his sire, certainly proved that it's what's inside that counts. This extraordinary Northern Dancer nature was also responsible, in part, for saving the life of Nureyev, another of Northern Dancer's offspring.

The pursuit of Northern Dancer progeny began in earnest the year following The Minstrel's Derby. Greek shipping magnate Stavros Niarchos dispatched his agent to the July 1978 Keeneland sales, and he returned to France (where Niarchos raced his horses) with a Northern Dancer colt out of the mare Special. The $1.3 million Niarchos paid was only the second time anyone had spent that much on a thoroughbred yearling at a public auction.

The first million-dollar yearling had been sold at the Keeneland sale two years earlier, a colt bought from Nelson Bunker Hunt by a group of Canadians. The colt's sire was Secretariat; his mother was the dam of champion racemare Dahlia. They called the colt Canadian Bound. (Those arguing that $1 million plus was a ridiculous amount to gamble on a horse so young it hadn't even had a saddle on its back were vindicated when Canadian Bound retired from racing with earnings of $4,770.)

Niarchos named his million-dollar yearling Nureyev, and the colt more than justified his investment; but by the time Northern Dancer retired from stud, 54 of his daughters and sons had sold at public auction for at least $1 million each.

As a two-year-old Nureyev ranked second in France's juvenile division; he won the English Two Thousand Guineas, but his jockey was disqualified; and he was the French champion miler at three. In 1981, he returned to Kentucky to stand at Walmac Farm. Like so many sons of Northern Dancer, he proved a sire of champions.

Nureyev's groom, Wayne Reinsmith, turned the feisty stallion out into his paddock after an early-morning breeding in May 1987. Five minutes later Nureyev was standing at the gate, holding up his right hind leg. Reinsmith realised, to his horror, that the leg was shattered – all that held it together was the hide.

It seems that Nureyev was feeling quite full of himself after the breeding, and kicked out with such a force that his leg became jammed between the planks of the fence. He managed to free himself and hobbled 20 yards back to the fence, where he waited for help.

Within minutes the Walmac staff was mobilised. Assistant farm manager Kenneth Aubrey phoned resident veterinarian and farm manager John Howard and then charged off to Nureyev's paddock, knowing only that the stallion had hurt himself.

'But when I saw his leg dangling and flopping like that I felt sick,' recalled Howard. 'I thought, Oh God, he's doomed. There's no hope.'

Like so many of Northern Dancer's offspring, Nureyev was tough, and in the end it was Nureyev's fighting spirit, and the dedication of Wayne Reinsmith, Kenneth Aubrey and John Howard – who virtually lived with the horse 24 hours a day for the next seven months – that brought about one of the most dramatic recoveries in thoroughbred history.

Nureyev was in shock; nonetheless, he hopped up the ramp of the horse ambulance on his three good legs. He must have had a sense of his danger, and been prepared to do whatever his human handlers asked.

At the Hagyard-Davidson-McGee Veterinary Hospital, X-rays confirmed the dismal diagnosis; the pain had sent Nureyev into a wild fit of terror. There was only a slight chance that surgery would work; moreover, when horses regain consciousness after surgery they are often so frightened that they flail about, incurring even greater damage. Many a horse has been 'humanely' put down under circumstances less critical.

John Howard had to make a decision, and make it quickly. Determined to do everything possible for the horse, Howard opted to risk the surgery. The anaesthetic was administered and eight people physically supported the 1,500-pound stallion as his knees buckled and he slowly sank to the ground. Once Nureyev was secured to the operating table built into the floor, it was raised by a hydraulic system.

Four surgeons worked on Nureyev for the next hour. They inserted two bone screws on each side of the break to form a double X. Next, the entire area was encased in a large cast. A special sling was then wrapped under his gut and across his chest. (When Nureyev came to he would be hoisted upright to prevent him from putting his full weight on his broken leg.)

He was then wheeled into a small stall and laid on his side. As Nureyev began to regain consciousness, Reinsmith and Aubrey sat on either side of his head, talking to him, reassuring him, although being so close to any horse coming out of an anaesthetic can be dangerous. In the case of a stallion with the aggressive temperament of Nureyev, there was no telling what might happen.

Before long Nureyev wanted to get up on his feet. The men tried to anticipate and support his every move. With Reinsmith and Aubrey calming Nureyev as the weary stallion struggled to stand, Howard co-ordinated the sling to support him. The first couple of times they raised him Nureyev was too weak to continue, so they slowly released the sling to allow him to lie down again. On the third try – about half an hour after the operation – Nureyev was able to stand.

Nureyev would spend the next five months in the sling. There was not one moment, day or night, during the entire recovery period that at least one of the three men was not by his side.

For the 48 hours following the surgery Nureyev seemed to recover well. Then intense pain undermined his will to live, and the fire in his eyes began to fade.

Nureyev might have been prepared to quit, but Howard, Reinsmith and Aubrey weren't: if they could get him angry enough to fight them, he might just stay angry enough to live.

For the next few days the trio took turns harassing Nureyev, hollering at him and slapping him. Years later, with Nureyev standing by them alive and well, the men still appeared pained at the memory of that time.

'I felt really terrible,' recounted Dr Howard, 'but we felt that if we could get his temper up he would live.'

And it worked. Like Northern Dancer, Nureyev didn't take kindly to being pushed around. After three days, the fire in his eyes returned: he was angry enough to take on all three of them.

The battle was far from over. It was May, and 90 per cent of the patients at the clinic were mares, many in season. Nureyev wanted to be out and breeding, and because he couldn't he began fretting and losing weight. So they decided to build a barn for him, away from the mares, and for the next seven months this small building was home to Nureyev, Reinsmith, Howard and Aubrey.

Nureyev began to improve and, supported by the sling, he was soon walking around the stall. But during the first week of June, when the team was changing his cast, they discovered that the leg was healing well except at one of the incision sites: there they found considerable fluid, a sign of infection.

The leg was cleaned, a new cast created, and the suspicious fluid sent off to be cultured. However, Nureyev also developed a respiratory problem, went off his feed and became depressed. Just as the antibiotics were stabilising him by boosting his immune system things became more critical. A damp spot appeared on the cast: the infection had set in once again. If it found its way into the bone, there was no hope.

And then fate stepped in. The day the culture of the bacteria Dr Howard had sent to the laboratory returned, designated as enterococcus cloacae, he also received the latest copy of the *New England Journal of Medicine*. There, on the front page, was an article about this particular bacterium, at the time the second leading cause of infection-related deaths in US hospitals.

The authors of the article had developed a drug called ceftazidime to treat this infection in humans. Dr Howard decided to try it on Nureyev. For 21 days the drug was administered to Nureyev, at the cost of $400 a day.

No sooner had the drug begun to clear up the infection than a new crisis loomed. The confinement and the pain had eroded the physical reserves of this once great champion runner. He would lay his weary head on the lap of whoever was closest. His temperature had risen to 103 degrees Fahrenheit; he had stopped eating and was showing signs of colic. If it took hold, he would certainly die. Immediately Nureyev was given electrolytes and nutrients intravenously. After several long days and nights, he began to brighten and his appetite returned.

Being on his feet in the sling for two months, coupled with his brush with colic and the humid summer heat, began to sap whatever strength the stallion had left. It wasn't long before he stopped eating again and slumped in his sling.

Dr Howard decided that they had to run the risk of allowing Nureyev to lie down. They slid a large, eight-inch-thick rubber mat on the floor beside him, and slowly lowered him, inches at a time, with the hoist. Seconds after Nureyev was lying safely on his side he fell into a deep sleep.

'He was one very relieved horse,' recalled Wayne Reinsmith. 'You could see that he was dreaming. Dreaming of running free.'

While Nureyev slept, all three men lay down in the stall with him, patting and reassuring him. When he woke up they slowly hoisted him in the sling back on his feet. For the next several weeks whenever he wanted to lie down, he signalled by staring at the men in the adjoining room and slumping in the sling.

The cast was changed almost every week, and all seemed to be going well, when Nureyev leapt back while being hoisted up and landed on his injured leg. Wild-eyed, Nureyev started to hyperventilate and appeared to be going into shock.

Dr Howard immediately administered drugs to ease the pain, removed the new cast, and X-rayed the break and surrounding area. Although the screws were effectively holding the bone together while it mended, two of the inch-long screw heads had broken off with the impact. The loose pieces, which were causing pressure and extreme pain, were removed.

As autumn approached, the cast was removed to prevent the muscles in the leg from atrophying, and Nureyev was fitted with a brace. By mid-September they could take him outside for brief walks without the sling, and eventually even the brace was removed. The final test came the day they allowed Nureyev to lie down unassisted.

'It was a tense moment for all of us,' said Dr Howard. 'It was as if everything was happening in slow motion. But he did it.'

If Dr Howard had any doubts that Nureyev was returning to his former feisty self, they were dispelled on 9 October. Nureyev lashed out with his once shattered hind leg, connected with Dr Howard's outstretched right arm, and broke it. Although stunned by the pain, Dr Howard had to laugh.

On 15 December Nureyev returned to Walmac, where a special complex had been built for him. Larger than most homes, the building contained a stall about three or four times normal size; an indoor arena, where he could be walked in inclement weather; a tack room; and his breeding parlour. Adjoining the barn was his own grassy paddock, where Wayne Reinsmith would spend long hours with him each day while the stallion leisurely grazed.

Late in the year, when it became evident that Nureyev would recover, a member of Nureyev's syndicate, Barry Weisbord, presented Lloyd's of London with a highly unusual proposition.

Weisbord held four and a half shares in Nureyev, for which he had paid $900,000 a share, and was covered for full mortality. The devotion of the men at Walmac to Nureyev's recovery inspired Weisbord to come up with a plan that he hoped would encourage other thoroughbred owners to do everything possible to save the lives of horses that appeared hopeless cases.

Nureyev's life was no longer in serious danger, but the question remained whether he would be able to resume breeding. Weisbord persuaded Lloyd's of London to switch the mortality insurance to live-foal insurance. He was gambling, essentially, that not only would the horse live, but he would also return to form as one of the world's leading stallions.

On 1 April 1988, almost a year after Nureyev shattered his right rear leg, the French mare, Histoire, was led into his breeding parlour. By the fall of 1990, Nureyev was the leading American-based sire of winners in Great Britain and Ireland, the leading sire of two-year-olds in Great Britain and Ireland, and fourth in the world as sire of two-year-olds.

Among Nureyev's offspring was the remarkably talented and tough Mièsque. Winner of the French One Thousand Guineas, Mièsque was champion seven times in England and France, and declared Champion Grass Mare in consecutive years in the United States. Nureyev's Irish-bred son, Theatrical, was Champion Grass Horse in the United States, and US-bred Zilzal was named English Horse of the Year.

More Valuable than Gold

By 1980, the year Nureyev was French champion, the Northern Dancer bloodline, a tidal wave to come, was clearly visible on the distant horizon. Like a little pebble tossed into a large pond, Northern Dancer created a few ripples at first. But 15 years after he entered stud, the ripples were fanning out wider and wider, and threatening the entire pond. It was as if he possessed some mystical quality that not only transformed seemingly ordinary horses into magnificent warriors, but also endowed them with the power to pass on the magic.

Lyphard, the colt Vincent O'Brien had turned down in 1970 because of his size, was the first of Northern Dancer's sons to be regarded as a great sire. It seemed appropriate that he was the first, since Lyphard was a carbon copy of Northern Dancer.

Lyphard's daughters were particularly spectacular: Three Troikas, who won the 1979 Prix de l'Arc de Triomphe, was named Horse of the Year in France, and declared French champion again in 1980. In 1978, Reine de Saba was Champion Filly in France, while Dancing Maid was Champion Three-year-old Filly in England. Two years earlier, Durtal was Champion Two-year-old Filly in England.

The presence of many of Nijinsky II's foals was also being felt. From his first crop came French-classic winner Green Dancer and Irish-classic winner Caucasus. In 1977, Cherry Hinton was Champion Two-year-old Filly in England. The following year, Ile de Bourbon won the King George VI and Queen Elizabeth Diamond Stakes. In 1979, Princess Lida was the Champion Two-year-old Filly in France. And Czarevitch was proving himself a formidable opponent on the dirt tracks of the United States.

Northern Dancer was 19. Although he was as potent as ever, his breeding days had to be numbered. Since some of his offspring appeared capable of passing on his extraordinary genes, their value skyrocketed: the hunt for the next great Northern Dancer was on.

It was becoming clear, however, that Nijinsky was an exception: the majority of the Northern Dancer bloodline inherited their sire's small stature. As there was no way of knowing which of Northern Dancer's offspring were blessed with his potency, thoroughbred owners decided to buy them all.

The market-place for his yearlings was the July sales at Kentucky's Keeneland, and the team of Robert Sangster, Vincent O'Brien and John Magnier appeared bent on cornering the Northern Dancer market. In the spring of 1980, Vincent O'Brien had five Northern Dancer two-year-olds in training, including Storm Bird, a million-dollar purchase the previous year, and five Nijinsky II two-year-olds.

By the summer of 1980 the bidding battles for Northern Dancer youngsters had become intense – and expensive. Sir Philip Payne-Gallwey, acting on behalf of Stavros Niarchos, went toe to toe with Robert Sangster for a Lyphard yearling; Payne-Gallwey emerged triumphant at a record-setting $1.7 million. Dolly Green, an oil heiress from California, paid $1.4 million for a Northern Dancer colt; and Robert Sangster won a full brother to The Minstrel for $1.25 million. When the sales chits were added up, 13 Northern Dancer yearlings had been bought for more than $7 million.

No one could have predicted what would happen next: it was like an old western movie. In the previous few years, when Robert Sangster and his gang rode into town almost everyone shuffled on to the sidelines. One glimpse of Sangster's steely determination told you that he was there to win. When he set his sights on a particular horse, he raised the price beyond the reach of ordinary millionaires, for he had seemingly endless wealth. Generally, he left town with exactly what he wanted.

And then, one July afternoon in 1981, a mysterious stranger came to town.

His name was Sheik Mohammed bin Rashid al Maktoum, of Dubai. His personal Boeing 727 was parked on the tarmac of Lexington's Blue Grass Field directly across the road from

Keeneland. In fact, it was impossible to drive into Keeneland's grounds without seeing the giant silver plane with United Arab Emirates painted on its body in English and Arabic. Its presence was a portent of things to come, as was its owner, the 31-year-old Arab prince.

There were two exceptional sons of Northern Dancer being offered at the sale: one was out of South Ocean, the other out of Sweet Alliance. Prior to the sale Sangster and Sheik Mohammed had sent advance parties to Windfields to scout these two colts.

On paper, the South Ocean colt appeared to be the better bet. South Ocean, bred and born of Windfields stock, was a stakes winner and had beaten Fanfreluche in the Canadian Oaks. She was also the dam of Canadian champion Northernette, and of Storm Bird, Champion Two-year-old in England and Ireland the previous year. Sangster and associates owned Storm Bird, who was trained by Vincent O'Brien, and they were not leaving town without Storm Bird's one-year-old brother.

They were particularly eager to buy this colt because of the promise Storm Bird had shown. At two he won all four of his races in Ireland and defeated a formidable field, headed by Tor-Agori-Mou, in the Dewhurst Stakes at Newmarket. In the spring of 1981, Storm Bird was favoured to win the Two Thousand Guineas, when one night a former Ballydoyle employee apparently crept into Storm Bird's stall and chopped all the hair from the animal's mane and tail. Following the trauma, Storm Bird became ill, and now, in the summer of 1981, still had not entered a race. In fact he only competed once that year, mid-September in France, where he finished a dismal seventh.

Soon after the bidding for this full brother to Storm Bird began everyone except Sangster and Sheik Mohammed dropped out: Sangster, it seemed, had met his match. No matter how far Sangster went, Sheik Mohammed raised the stakes. Up and up the prices went. One million. Two million. Three million. Three million four hundred thousand, offered Sheik Mohammed. Three million five hundred thousand, replied Sangster. Having pushed Robert Sangster into paying more than twice the previous record for a thoroughbred yearling, Sheik Mohammed walked calmly away.

He obviously hadn't left the battle because the stakes were too high: 20 minutes later he outduelled American Will Farish, paying $3.3 million for the Northern Dancer colt out of Sweet Alliance.

The colt, which he named Shareef Dancer, was Champion Three-year-old Colt in England and Ireland in 1983, and was syndicated for $40 million.

The $3.5 million for Storm Bird's full brother, however, wasn't a great blow to Sangster and the company coffers. While in Lexington he was also negotiating with US interests for a $30 million syndication of Storm Bird. Sangster stated after the sale that he had been prepared to go even higher than $3.5 million: 'When we shoot, we hit. He's a full brother to a champion colt and a fantastic filly. Like anything else in the world, the best things in life have a value. We estimated that he will make at least $2.7 million at the track as a racehorse.'

They optimistically named the colt Ballydoyle, after O'Brien's training centre. Unfortunately the horse was not disposed to be either a racehorse or a stallion.

Until this sale, Robert Sangster had dominated the Keeneland summer sales; he bought Northern Dancer yearlings as if he had the entire Bank of England in his wallet. Sheik Mohammed's fortunes, however, were backed by oil. One of seven sheikdoms that form the United Arab Emirates, Dubai was second to Abu Dhabi in oil reserves. At the time crude oil was selling for $35.93 a barrel and Dubai was producing between 300,000 and 400,000 barrels daily.

Sangster, at 45, was the sole heir to Vernon's, the football-pools business in Liverpool upon which his father had founded the family fortune. During his national service, the stocky five-foot-nine-inch Sangster was boxing champion of his regiment. And it appeared that these days he enjoyed the combative atmosphere of the sales ring.

Sheik Mohammed bin Rashid al Maktoum, the third son of the ruler of Dubai, had attended Cambridge, 'about twenty minutes from Newmarket. I went to the races there. Racing is in my blood.'

'The thoroughbred came from three Arabian stallions,' he explained. 'My people used to breed horses to save their lives. Now we breed to race.'

Indeed, during the mid-seventeenth century British racehorse breeders imported Arabian horses to breed with their racing stock, often cobs derived of breeds from Galloway ponies to Italian and Spanish imports. The elegant Arabian horse was not only agile and quick, but the purest-bred horse in the world. All 750,000 modern thoroughbreds trace their direct male line to only three sires – the Byerley Turk, the Darley Arabian, and the Godolphin Arabian.

Just as the Arabian horse altered the racehorse at the turn of the eighteenth century, an Arab prince would play a lead role in the dramatic events that altered the destiny of thoroughbred racing in the twentieth century.

When Robert Sangster and his gang rode into town next year, the young Arab prince would not be far behind.

There seemed no way, short of kidnapping Northern Dancer, to corner the entire market of his yearlings, until the autumn of 1981, when a wire arrived at Windfields' Oshawa farm: 'ON BEHALF OF DR LASLO URBAN WE BEG TO GIVE $40,000,000 US FOR THE FULL PROPERTY OF THE STALLION NORTHERN DANCER BAY 1961 NEARCTIC OUT OF NATALMA STOP PLEASE ADVISE IF INTERESTED STOP REGARDS.' The wire was signed Horse France, a Paris-based bloodstock agency.

E.P. Taylor had suffered a debilitating stroke in the autumn of 1980, and his son, Charles, a former foreign correspondent, author and passionate racing man, assumed leadership of Windfields. The wire arrived just as he, farm manager Peter Poole and vice-president Joe Thomas were reviewing the results of that year's yearling sales.

Northern Dancer was 20 years old.

'You can imagine how taken aback we were,' recalled Charles. 'Forty million dollars was unheard-of money for a horse, especially one so old.'

Dr Urban was a French veterinarian who had bid $120,000 at the 1977 Keeneland sale for a colt by Northern Dancer out of Two Rings. He was a small colt, and Dr Urban was the only bidder. The colt was Northern Baby; he won the Champion Stakes, was third in the Epsom Derby, and had recently been syndicated for $12 million.

Charles continued:

> At first we laughed. It simply sounded too fantastic. We went over to the golf club to have some lunch and to work on other farm business, but the telegram wouldn't leave our minds. So, we decided we had better take it seriously. When we got back to the farm we did two things. We began informing all the other syndicate members, and we replied to the cable. We asked who Dr Urban was representing and where they proposed to stand Northern Dancer if the offer was accepted.
>
> That second point was the most important consideration. They, whoever 'they' were, might easily have wanted to move

the horse to Europe or even to the Middle East. At Northern Dancer's age we wouldn't have wanted to move him from the place he'd spent a very happy half of his life.

The reaction of the other members of the syndicate was mixed. Some were adamant against selling, some were bemused and didn't know which way they'd go, and some were anxious to sell. That surprised us. Right from the beginning I had been able to say, 'No way!' I couldn't imagine selling him – he was family.

My mother was convinced that Northern Dancer recognised her when she came to give him sugar cubes. Maybe it was only the sugar cubes, I don't know, but that's the way we all felt about him.

Another great concern was his health. We just weren't certain that he could survive the move to wherever they wanted to take him – they never did answer the questions we asked in our wire.

Another reason for rejecting the offer, believe it or not, was financial. Forty million, as high as it sounded, might not have been enough for him at the time, especially in a rising market.

Each of the 32 shares in Northern Dancer was now worth $1.25 million, and enough shareholders were in favour of selling that the Taylor family had a dilemma.

'In spite of our own attitude,' recalled Charles, 'we decided to remain neutral, out of fairness to the others. We decided not to cast our nine votes. If all the rest of the syndicate members wanted to sell we would throw our shares in with them, and if Dr Urban then came up with the $40 million, well, the horse would have been his.'

For days the telephone wires burned, as the most firmly convinced shareholders on each side of the debate attempted to sway the others. One shareholder was so adamantly opposed that he threatened to take out an injunction to block the sale.

Eighteen shareholders voted to sell Northern Dancer, one abstained, and five shareholders voted against selling. Charles Taylor added his nine votes to the five opposed.

Windfields notified Dr Urban that they could not deliver the 'whole horse', but did furnish him with the names and addresses of all shareholders so he could contact each individually. In theory Dr Urban could have bought the 18 shares held by those who had voted to sell Northern Dancer. There was, however, a clause in the syndication giving members the right of first refusal on any share being sold by matching the offer.

Dr Urban wired a simple 'JE SUIS DESOLE'. His only comment to the European press was that he could not understand how anyone could have refused the offer.

'To some of us,' said Charles, 'Northern Dancer was more than a horse. There are those who believe that everything has a price – but not Northern Dancer.'

Now that the sale of Northern Dancer had been thwarted, the focus returned to purchasing his offspring at public auction. Yet if someone was willing to pay $40 million for the ageing stallion, how far would they go to purchase his yearlings?

19 JULY 1983

Northern Dancer was asleep, stretched out on a thick bed of straw in his Maryland stall. It was late evening and the only sounds to break the still night air were the occasional snorts and grunts of his stable-mates.

Six hundred miles to the west, however, in the sales pavilion at the Keeneland, the atmosphere was anything but tranquil. It was more like the OK Corral. Rumour had it there was about to be a major shoot-out between the Englishman and the Arab prince.

Sheik Mohammed had returned to the Keeneland sales in 1982, and once again dogged Sangster's bids on a Nijinsky II colt. Sangster had to go to $4.2 million to get what he wanted. As before, Sheik Mohammed calmly walked away.

Some believed Sangster was showing Sheik Mohammed that this was still his town. They thought Sangster was flexing his financial muscle. Others, however, suspected that the Arab prince was simply toying with the wealthy British scrapper, letting him win, but determining the price. The time would soon come, they were sure, when the prince would play his hand.

There was definitely something in the air. Prior to the sale Keeneland officials requested that the public stay away. 'We're asking the general public to please refrain from attending,' said Keeneland publicist Jim Williams. 'We don't have the facilities . . . We're concerned about the safety of the buyers and sellers.'

What better way to assure a crowd? The spectators came in droves to witness the spectacle.

The horse at the centre of this showdown was a striking-looking bay son of Northern Dancer out of the mare My Bupers.

At 11 p.m. the colt was led from the stables into the walking ring behind the sales building. Robert Sangster and his group, which included Stavros Niarchos, Vincent O'Brien, O'Brien's brother Phonsie and about twenty other agents, partners and relatives, were gathered at the back of the pavilion. They were ready to pay $5.8 million for the colt – more, if need be.

The drama heightened when Sheik Mohammed, who generally bid from his reserved seats at the front of the arena, also moved to the back. He and his entourage chose to stand next to a partition, out of sight of Robert Sangster and his group.

When the Northern Dancer colt was led into the ring, a tense hush fell over the pavilion. The auctioneer gave his preamble on the colt's pedigree and the contest began.

The opening bid was $1 million, and in no time it had soared to $4 million. There was a brief pause. Then a new world record, $4.5 million, was hit. At $5.2 million everyone faded to the sidelines except Sangster and Sheik Mohammed. When the bidding surpassed $6 million, Sangster and his team conferred after every bid – they were beyond their agreed limit.

On the other side of the partition Sheik Mohammed stood silently. His attention was focused on the horse in the ring and the electronic board that monitored the prices. His face showed absolutely no expression.

Every time Sangster raised the stakes, Colonel Richard Warden, Sheik Mohammed's chief bloodstock adviser, immediately countered with a higher bid.

At $8 million the pressure was reflected in the faces of Sangster and his associates. Finally, by increasing his personal financial commitment to the partnership agreement, Sangster got consensus to go as far as $10 million.

The bidding continued until Sangster went to $9.5 million. Leaning against the wooden divider, Sheik Mohammed fixed his eyes on the bidding board. His personal secretary, John Leat, nodded to Warden, who looked up at the ceiling, muttered something, and raised the bid to $9.6 million.

There was a brief pause before Philip Payne-Gallwey, doing the bidding for the Sangster group, countered with an even $10 million.

The audience was stunned. The price had literally 'gone off the board' – the seven-digit electronic board could not accommodate an eight-digit bid and there was a slight delay while they rolled the board back to zero.

Warden took the bid to $10.2 million. Sangster was ready to go to $10.5 million: he was sure that Sheik Mohammed would give up and walk away as he had in the past. Sangster's team disagreed. Their collective 'horse sense' told them that no matter how far they went, they weren't going to win this battle.

'Going once. Going twice. Sold. For $10.2 million!' The show-down was over; the opponents holstered their smoking wallets, and the prize was led back to his stable. The audience in the hot, steamy pavilion stood and applauded the performance. There would not be an encore.

As soon as the purchase ticket was signed Sheik Mohammed and his party moved quickly though the excited crowd. The prince remained silent in face of the reporters and photographers; but his secretary was exuberant: 'We got him! We got him!' he said, laughing, as the party headed to the door.

Robert Sangster and his team took refuge in the Keeneland bar. Although disappointed, Sangster cheerfully commented, 'It's good for the thoroughbred industry and good for us. If this one is worth $10 million, four of the ones we have have to be worth $40 million.'

When the dust settled at the end of the sale, 11 sons and daughters of 22-year-old Northern Dancer had sold for at least $1 million each.

Sheik Mohammed's colt, called Snaafi Dancer, didn't race. He was also a failure at stud.

Story without an End

It had been 20 years since Northern Dancer's breathtaking charge down the stretch at Churchill Downs, and now British racing fans at the Epsom Derby were in for a double thrill. Not one, but two Northern Dancer colts were flying up the stretch: El Gran Senor and Secreto were matching each other, stride for stride, will for will. Their heads bobbing on every other beat, they were soaring toward the finish in such perfect harmony that they appeared to be one. Neither would concede. And when they flew past the world's most famous finish post these two extraordinary animals, were indeed, one.

After contemplating the photo of the finish, the racing stewards eventually declared Secreto the winner. Secreto's muzzle was fractionally higher than El Gran Senor's.

Although Secreto's name was inscribed in the ledger as the winner of the 1984 Derby, both horses had won. Traditionally, the Derby winner's owner, trainer and entourage are invited to the Royal Box. This year the Queen Mother extended her invitation to everyone involved with both horses.

It was indeed a family affair. Not only were El Gran Senor and Secreto sons of Northern Dancer, they had both been bred and born at Windfields; El Gran Senor was trained by Vincent O'Brien, and Secreto was trained by Vincent's 27-year-old son, David.

Since 1970, Nijinsky, The Minstrel and now Secreto (and El Gran Senor) had won this, the race that defines the thoroughbred. Thus the thoroughbred was becoming redefined in the image of Northern Dancer, the little horse no one wanted to buy because he didn't look like a thoroughbred.

Northern Dancer's domination had become easily recognised now that so many of his offspring were dams and sires of great champions. The winner's circle at Epsom would now feature this next generation.

It had begun two years earlier, on Wednesday, 2 June 1982. Northern Dancer's big strapping grandson, Golden Fleece, was galloping leisurely near the back of the pack as the Derby field thundered down Tattenham Hill at Epsom. Although this son of Nijinsky was the favourite, he seemed in no hurry – either to win or reward the fans who had backed him. At Tattenham Corner Golden Fleece had only three horses behind him; up ahead the leaders were blasting down the straight. No horse had come from that far off the pace to win.

Then, suddenly inspired, Golden Fleece leapt forward through the pack. He tore down the stretch, his long legs flying, his hooves barely touching Epsom's turf. Four horses were bunched together on the rail, battling for the lead. Golden Fleece let up briefly and jockey Pat Eddery calmly steered the colt to the outside. There, with clear going, he flew past the remaining horses, up the rise and across the finish. At 2:35.27 seconds Golden Fleece had run the fastest Derby since the installation of electronic-timing equipment at Epsom in 1964, and only a fraction off the hand-timed record of 2:33.8 seconds set by Mahmoud in 1936.

That autumn saw the beginning of a shift in the perception of Northern Dancer's international dominance. Five direct descendants of Northern Dancer won or placed in the seven inaugural Breeders' Cup races at California's Hollywood Park; moreover, grandson Chief's Crown won the Juvenile and was voted Champion Two-year-old in the United States.

Not that long ago thoroughbred experts had been convinced that the Northern Dancer bloodline lacked the stamina to win races in Europe and Great Britain until Nijinsky, The Minstrel, Nureyev and the rest proved them wrong. Then it was assumed that Northern Dancer offspring could not handle North America's oval dirt tracks. Chief's Crown was the first of many to disabuse the sceptics on that score; and whereas North American thoroughbred farms had bred Northern Dancers for export to Europe, now the bloodline was considered suitable to the domestic market as well. Chief's Crown was from the first crop of Northern Dancer's son Danzig. Although lightly raced because of an injury, Danzig was very much like his sire, and would prove the leading stallion in the US for years to come.

The first of Northern Dancer's descendants to win the Kentucky Derby, on 3 May 1986, was Ferdinand, the chestnut son of Nijinsky II. Riding this Northern Dancer grandson was Bill Shoemaker, more than twenty years after he had turned down the opportunity to ride Northern Dancer – and finished second to him – in the Kentucky Derby.

A month later a pair of Northern Dancer grandsons finished one-two in the Epsom Derby: the winner, Shahrastani, was a son of Nijinsky II; Dancing Brave, a son of Lyphard, was second. Dancing Brave went on to win the Prix de l'Arc de Triomphe. (A great-grandson, Bering, was second.) Both Shahrastani and Dancing Brave were champions. Northern Dancer was obviously passing on his dynamic genetic elixir to his offspring, and they to theirs.

It was, no doubt, partly due to his 'super-genes' that Northern Dancer continued to breed and impregnate mares for as long as he did. Very few thoroughbred stallions live past 25, let alone still breed. At 25, Northern Dancer was the equivalent of a 70-year-old man. Shareholders in the stallion had their brood mares lined up at the door. There were offers of $1 million for a single breeding, with no guarantee of a live foal.

By mid-April, Northern Dancer had covered 24 mares, almost twice the number he'd been asked to cover two years earlier. He had been breeding a mare a day. (When he was younger he could easily handle two, but age and the heavy workload was leaving him tired, slower and frustrated.)

In the past he had dragged his handlers the 50 yards between his stall and the breeding arena, dancing, often on his hind legs, snorting and hollering. Now he merely pranced. In the wild he would have been deposed by now, and it's not unreasonable to assume that he understood he was beyond his prime. And the results of the breedings weren't promising. He had impregnated only four of the mares, and only two would produce foals.

As Charles Taylor explained:

> The staff had been monitoring him very closely and they called in several experts from the New Bolton Centre. They were standing around the microscope, dressed in white lab coats, shaking their heads. When I looked down the microscope, it looked like there was a riot going on. But in actual fact, his sperm count was very low.
>
> My own perspective was not all that scientific. It seemed to

me that his heart simply wasn't in it. That he looked almost embarrassed.

I made the decision to retire him, and immediately informed the other shareholders. But all the time I was wondering: how's he going to take it? All these years he has thought every mare on the farm was for him, so I was concerned how he would react.

But it didn't bother him. I think he was relieved.

By the time of his retirement, the Northern Dancer tidal wave had washed over the entire planet: from Japan to South Africa, through Europe and the British Isles, and back to Canada and the US. His sons and daughters were the pre-eminent breeding stock; his grandsons and granddaughters the élite among racehorses.

The following spring the next wave of Northern Dancers began to appear in the Epsom Derby winner's circle: on 1 June 1988, a great-grandson, Kahyasi, sired by Ile de Bourbon, a son of Nijinsky II, became the seventh of the Northern Dancer line to win this race of races. And many more of his descendants would not only dominate the Derby field, but the majority of the classic races the world over. For this little horse, discounted over and over again, surely had become the patriarch of the modern thoroughbred.

16 NOVEMBER 1990
CHESAPEAKE BAY, MARYLAND, USA

Northern Dancer died at 6.15 a.m., a mere six weeks after I visited him in Maryland and 'interviewed' him for this book. Charles Taylor had received a call at dinnertime the previous evening, alerting him that Northern Dancer had come down with colic and that the veterinarian, Alan McCarthy, was treating him and would stay with him throughout the night. McCarthy and the staff were very concerned, and once again called in the experts at the New Bolton Centre for assistance.

'I was taken a bit by surprise,' said Taylor. 'We had discovered several years earlier that Northern Dancer had a slight heart murmur, so I guess I had been preparing myself that when he died it would be a heart attack.'

Charles continued to receive telephone calls every couple of hours until midnight, when, to everyone's relief, Northern Dancer was no longer in the great distress he had suffered earlier that evening.

'I went to bed feeling very hopeful,' continued Taylor.

He was wakened at 6 a.m. by the telephone. The colic had returned and Northern Dancer was in tremendous pain. McCarthy and the New Bolton vets had considered all the options. Operating would be the most hopeful course of action, but there were too many considerations.

Taking into account his distress and the fact that he had not been in a horse van for years, it was deemed too great a risk to trailer him to a clinic. Given his age and his heart murmur, they weren't certain whether he could handle the anaesthetic, let alone the operation.

After listening to the latest prognosis, Taylor concurred that Northern Dancer should no longer have to suffer, and agreed to have him 'put out of his misery'. When Taylor hung up the telephone Northern Dancer was given the fatal injection.

In Canada, Northern Dancer's death was treated by the media like that of a popular head of state: it was on the front page of every major newspaper from coast to coast and the lead story on national television and radio. It had been more than 26 years since he had brought the nation to its feet as he'd steamed down the stretch at Churchill Downs, and 22 years since the little Canadian hero and Athlete of the Year had been shipped to the US, yet his death was mourned with sincerity and dignity.

Most of us remembered not only Northern Dancer's Derby, but where and with whom we watched the race. That joyful memory had made us smile, made us proud. His death saddened us.

Windfields Farm was inundated with phone calls, cables and letters of condolence from around the globe.

'It was really amazing,' said Windfields' general manager Bernard McCormack, 'the number of people who were genuinely upset at his passing. And it was very touching. I remember one woman calling from a pay phone in Alberta, the other side of the country. She had just heard the news on the radio in her car. She was in tears – as, of course, was everyone on this farm.'

Arrangements had been made with the Canadian Department of Agriculture to bring Northern Dancer back to Canada when he died. An oak casket had been built, and when the necessary border-crossing papers had been processed, a van carrying Northern Dancer's body set out to bring him home. Charles Taylor, Bernard McCormack and Windfields Farm veterinarian Patrick Hearn drove the 150 miles from Windfields to the Thousand Islands border crossing to meet the van and escort it to the farm.

It was midnight, cold and raining when they arrived back at Windfields. The entire farm staff had congregated to pay their last respects.

Northern Dancer was buried in the heart of Windfields Farm, midway between the barn where he was born and the barn where he began his days as a stallion.

The Champions

Northern Dancer sired 635 foals over 23 seasons. Eighty per cent (511) of these animals raced, of which 80 per cent (410) were winners. Of his 146 stakes winners, 26 were declared champion in Ireland, England, France, Italy, the United States or Canada. The champions are listed chronologically according to their foaling year.

VICEREGAL (1966) chestnut colt – Victoria Regina by Menetrier
  Horse of the Year – Canada 1968
  Champion Two-year-old Colt – Canada 1968

  Major races:
  Coronation Futurity – Canada 1968
  Cup and Saucer Stakes – Canada 1968
  Summer Stakes – Canada 1968
  Vandal Stakes – Canada 1968
  Victoria Stakes – Canada 1968
  Clarendon Stakes – Canada 1968
  Colin Stakes – Canada 1968
  Whitney Purse (3rd) – United States 1969

ONE FOR ALL (1966) bay colt – Quill by Princequillo
  Champion Grass Horse – Canada 1970

  Major races:
  Sunset Handicap – United States 1970
  Pan American Handicap – United States 1970
  Canadian International Championship – Canada 1971
  Niagara Handicap – Canada 1971
  Canadian Int'l Championship (2nd) – Canada 1969
  Pan American Handicap (3rd) – United States 1971
  Leonard Richards Stakes (3rd) – United States 1969

DANCE ACT (1966) chestnut gelding – Queens Stature by Le Lavandou
  Champion Handicap Horse – Canada 1971

Champion Handicap Horse – Canada 1970
Champion Older Horse – Canada 1970

Major races:
Dominion Day Handicap – Canada 1971
Jockey Club Cup – Canada 1970
Horometer Stakes – Canada 1970
Durham Cup – Canada 1970
Eclipse Handicap – Canada 1971
Seagram Cup – Canada 1971
Fair Play Stakes – Canada 1971

NIJINSKY II (1967) bay colt – Flaming Page by Bull Page
Horse of the Year – England 1970
Champion Three-year-old Colt – England 1970
Champion Three-year-old Colt – Ireland 1970
Champion Two-year-old Colt – England 1969
Champion Two-year-old Colt – Ireland 1969

Major races:
Two Thousand Guineas – England 1970
Epsom Derby – England 1970
St Leger – England 1970
King George VI & Queen Elizabeth Stakes – England 1970
Irish Sweeps Derby – Ireland 1970
Gladness Stakes – Ireland 1970
Dewhurst Stakes – England 1969
Railway Stakes – Ireland 1969
Beresford Stakes – Ireland 1969
Prix de l'Arc de Triomphe (2nd) – France 1970
Champion Stakes (2nd) – England 1970

FANFRELUCHE (1967) bay filly – Giboulette by Chop Chop
Champion Three-year-old Filly – North America 1970
Horse of the Year – Canada 1970
Champion Three-year-old Filly – Canada 1970

Major races:
Manitoba Centennial Derby – Canada 1970
Alabama Stakes – United States 1970
Benson & Hedges Invitational – Canada 1970
Quebec Derby – Canada 1970
Bison City Stakes – Canada 1970
Selene Stakes – Canada 1970
Princess Elizabeth Stakes – Canada 1969
Natalma Stakes – Canada 1969
Queen's Plate (2nd) – Canada 1970
Spinster Stakes (2nd) – United States 1970
Canadian Oaks (2nd) – Canada 1970
Wonder Where Stakes (2nd) – Canada 1970

Gazelle Handicap (3rd) – United States 1970

MINSKY (1968) chestnut colt – Flaming Page by Bull Page
Champion Two-year-old Colt – Ireland 1970

Major races:
Beresford Stakes – Ireland 1970
Railway Stakes – Ireland 1970
Gladness Stakes – Ireland 1971
Tetrarch Stakes – Ireland 1971
Durham Cup – Canada 1971
Durham Cup – Canada 1973

LAURIES DANCER (1968) bay filly – Its Ann by Royal Gem II
Horse of the Year – Canada 1971
Champion Three-year-old Filly – Canada 1971

Major races:
Alabama Stakes – United States 1971
Delaware Oaks – United States 1971
Canadian Oaks – Canada 1971
Bison City Stakes – Canada 1971
Star Shoot Stakes – Canada 1971
Maple Leaf Stakes – Canada 1972
Manitoba Derby (3rd) – Canada 1971

NICE DANCER (1969) bay colt – Nice Princess by Beau Prince
Champion Three-year-old Colt – Canada 1972

Major races:
Manitoba Derby – Canada 1972
Breeders' Stakes – Canada 1972
Col. R.S. MacLaughlin Handicap – Canada 1972
Achievement Handicap – Canada 1972
Dominion Day Handicap – Canada 1973
Canadian Maturity Stakes – Canada 1973
Eclipse Handicap (2nd) – Canada 1973
Prince of Wales Stakes (3rd) – Canada 1972

BROADWAY DANCER (1972) bay filly – Broadway Melody by Tudor Melody
Champion Two-year-old Filly – France 1974

Major races:
Prix Morny – France 1974
Prix Robert Papin (2nd) – France 1974
Poule d'Essai des Pouliches (3rd) – France 1974

THE MINSTREL (1974) chestnut colt – Fleur by Victoria Park
Horse of the Year – England 1977
Horse of the Year – Ireland 1977

Major races:
Epsom Derby – England 1977
King George VI & Queen Elizabeth Stakes – England 1977
Irish Sweeps Derby – Ireland 1977
Ascot Two Thousand Guineas Trial Stakes – England 1977
Dewhurst Stakes – England 1976
Larkspur Stakes – Ireland 1976
Irish Two Thousand Guineas (2nd) – Ireland 1977
Two Thousand Guineas (3rd) – England 1977

DANCE IN TIME (1974) bay colt – Allegro by Chop Chop
Champion Three-year-old Colt – Canada 1977

Major races:
Prince of Wales Stakes – Canada 1977
Breeders' Stakes – Canada 1977
Friar Rock Stakes – Canada 1977
Cup and Saucer Stakes (3rd) – Canada 1976

NORTHERNETTE (1974) bay filly – South Ocean by New Providence
Champion Two-year-old Filly – Canada 1976
Champion Three-year-old Filly – Canada 1977

Major races:
Apple Blossom Handicap – United States 1978
Top Flight Handicap – United States 1978
Canadian Oaks – Canada 1977
Chrysanthemum Handicap – United States 1977
Selene Stakes – Canada 1977
Fury Stakes – Canada 1977
Mazarine Stakes – Canada 1976
Spinster Stakes (2nd) – United States 1978
Black Helen Handicap (2nd) – United States 1978
Queen's Plate (2nd) – Canada 1977
Test Stakes (2nd) – United States 1977
Star Shoot Stakes (2nd) – Canada 1977
Bison City Stakes (2nd) – Canada 1977
Princess Elizabeth Stakes (2nd) – Canada 1976

GIBOULEE (1974) bay colt – Victory Chant by Victoria Park
Champion Older Horse – Canada 1978

Major races:
Dominion Day Handicap – Canada 1978
Virgil Handicap – Canada 1978
Manitoba Derby – Canada 1977
Queen's Plate Trials – Canada 1977
Coronation Futurity – Canada 1976
Carleton Stakes – Canada 1976
Massachusetts Handicap (2nd) – United States 1978

Redoubt Handicap (2nd) – United States 1978
Flamingo Stakes (2nd) – United States 1977
Yearling Sales Stakes (2nd) – Canada 1976
Queen's Plate (3rd) – Canada 1977

TRY MY BEST (1975) bay colt – Sex Appeal by Buckpasser
Champion Two-year-old Colt – England 1977
Champion Two-year-old Colt – Ireland 1977
Champion Miler – Ireland 1978

Major races:
Larkspur Stakes – Ireland 1977
William Hill Dewhurst Stakes – England 1977
Vauxhall Trial Stakes – Ireland 1978

NUREYEV (1977) bay colt – Special by Forli
Champion Miler – France 1980

Major races:
Prix Djebel – France 1980
Prix Thomas Bryon – France 1979

STORM BIRD (1978) bay colt – South Ocean by New Providence
Champion Two-year-old Colt – Ireland 1980
Champion Two-year-old Colt – England 1980

Major races:
Anglesey Stakes – Ireland 1980
National Stakes – Ireland 1980
Larkspur Stakes – Ireland 1980
William Hill Dewhurst Stakes – England 1980

WOODSTREAM (1979) chestnut filly – Rule Formi by Forli
Champion Two-year-old Filly – Ireland 1981

Major races:
Moyglare Stud Stakes – Ireland 1981
William Hill Cheveley Park Stakes – Ireland 1981
Goffs Irish One Thousand Guineas (2nd) – Ireland 1982

SHAREEF DANCER (1980) bay colt – Sweet Alliance by Sir Ivor
Champion Three-year-old Colt – England 1983
Champion Three-year-old Colt – Ireland 1983

Major races:
King Edward VII Stakes – England 1983
Irish Sweeps Derby – Ireland 1983

DANZATORE (1980) bay colt – Shake A Leg by Raise A Native
Champion Two-year-old Colt – Ireland 1982

Major races:
Ashford Castle Stakes – Ireland 1982
Panasonic Beresford Stakes – Ireland 1982
The Minstrel Stakes – Ireland 1983

SECRETO (1981) bay colt – Betty's Secret by Secretariat
Champion Three-year-old Colt – Ireland 1984

Major races:
Ever Ready (Epsom) Derby Stakes – England 1984
Tetrarch Stakes – Ireland 1984
Irish Two Thousand Guineas (3rd) – Ireland 1984

EL GRAN SENOR (1981) bay colt – Sex Appeal by Buckpasser
Champion Three-year-old Colt – England 1984
Champion Miler – England 1984
Champion Two-year-old – England 1983
Champion Two-year-old – Ireland 1983

Major races:
General Accident Two Thousand Guineas – England 1984
Joe McGrath Irish Sweeps Derby – Ireland 1984
Gladness Stakes – Ireland 1984
William Hill Dewhurst Stakes – England 1983
P.J. Pendergast Railway Stakes – Ireland 1983
BBA/Goffs National Stakes – Ireland 1983
Ever Ready (Epsom) Derby Stakes (2nd) – England 1984

SADLER'S WELLS (1981) bay colt – Fairy Bridge by Bold Reason
Champion Miler – France 1984

Major races:
Airlie/Coolmore Two Thousand Guineas – Ireland 1984
Coral Eclipse Stakes – England 1984
Golden Fleece Phoenix Championship – Ireland 1984
Derrinstown Stud Stakes – Ireland 1984
Panasonic Beresford Stakes – Ireland 1983
Prix du Jockey-Club (2nd) – France 1984
Gladness Stakes (2nd) – Ireland 1984

ANTHEUS (1982) bay colt – Apachee by Sir Gaylord
Champion Older Horse – Italy 1986

Major races:
La Coupe de Maisons-Lafitte – France 1986
Del Jockey Club – Italy 1986
Prix de la Ville de Trouville – France 1985
La Coupe (2nd) – France 1986
Prix du Haras de Fresnay le Buffard (2nd) – France 1985
Prix Maurice de Nieuil (3rd) – France 1986

Prix Foy (3rd) – France 1986

ADJAL (1984) bay colt – Native Partner by Raise A Native
    Champion Sprinter – France 1987
    Champion Sprinter – England 1987

    Major races:
    Craven Stakes – England 1987
    Norcros July Cup – England 1987
    William Hill Sprint Championship – England 1987
    William Hill Dewhurst Stakes – England 1986

UNFUWAIN (1985) bay colt – Height of Fashion by Bustino
    Champion Three-year-old Colt – England 1988
    Champion Three-year-old Colt – France 1988

    Major races:
    Lanes End John Porter Stakes – England 1989
    General Accident Jockey Club Stakes – England 1989
    Warren Stakes – England 1988
    Dalham Chester Vase – England 1988
    Princess of Wales' Stakes – England 1988
    King George VI & Queen Elizabeth Diamond Stakes (2nd) – England 1988
    Prix de l'Arc de Triomphe (4th) – France 1988

Northern Dancer's Influence on Classic Races

Northern Dancer's legacy to thoroughbred racing is evident in the results of the élite races referred to as 'the Classics'. By 1994 the Northern Dancer line had become so dominant that a direct descendant of this extraordinary horse had either won or placed in nearly every one of the world's most important thoroughbred events.

It would require an entire volume to accommodate a complete listing of the top three placings of the Northern Dancer line in the classics. Instead we have simply chronicled the English, Irish, French (Prix du Jockey-Club) and Kentucky Derbys.

We have also included the Breeders' Cup races, in which the very best thoroughbreds from both sides of the Atlantic compete annually. In fact, Northern Dancer was indirectly responsible for the spectacular afternoon of magnificent horses and lavish purses known as Breeders' Cup Day.

By the early 1980s the megamillion-dollar battles being waged at the Keeneland sales to secure Northern Dancer yearlings were throwing the sport out of balance. While Northern Dancer's offspring consistently sold for 20 per cent above the average, the prices paid for the progeny of other stallions also became dangerously inflated. Breeders who had once worked to produce race horses now sought to produce revenue.

Stallion syndication and breeding fees skyrocketed, and yearlings were selling for far more than they could possibly win at the track. The market would of course eventually crash – everyone knew it – but it took a group of concerned thoroughbred breeders, spearheaded by John Gaines of Kentucky's Gainesway Farm, to confront the situation before the impending crash toppled the entire sport.

The plan was to showcase thoroughbred sport through live television coverage. Breeders were invited to pay subscription fees into a fund that would become the prize money for the races. The inaugural Breeders' Cup races were held on 10 November 1984 at California's Hollywood Park, offering $10 million in purses. The winner of the first race, the 1984 Breeders' Cup Sprint, was Eillo, a grandson of Northern Dancer and an omen of things to come.

EPSOM DERBY

1970	Nijinsky
1977	The Minstrel
1979	Northern Baby (3rd)
1982	Golden Fleece – grandson, by Nijinsky II
1984	Secreto
	El Gran Senor (2nd)
1986	Shahrastani – grandson, by Nijinsky II
	Dancing Brave (2nd) – grandson, by Lyphard
1987	Most Welcome (2nd) – grandson, by Be My Guest
1988	Kahyasi – great-grandson, by Ile de Bourbon by Nijinsky II
1990	Quest for Fame – great-grandson, out of Aryene by Green Dancer by Nijinsky II
	Blue Stag (2nd) – grandson, by Sadler's Wells
1991	Generous – great-grandson by Caerleon by Nijinsky II
	Marju (2nd) – great-grandson by Last Tycoon by Try My Best
	Star of Gdansk (3rd) – great-grandson, by Danzig Connection by Danzig
1992	Dr Devious – great-grandson, out of Rose of Jerico out of Rose Red
	St Jovite (2nd) – great-grandson, out of Northern Sunset by Northfields
1993	Commander-in-Chief – great-grandson, by Dancing Brave by Lyphard
1994	Erhaab – great-grandson, by Chief's Crown by Danzig
	King's Theatre (2nd) – grandson, by Sadler's Wells
	Colonel Collins (3rd) – grandson, by El Gran Senor
1995	Lammtarra – grandson, by Nijinsky II, out of Snow Bride, out of Awaasif, out of Royal Statute
	Tamure (2nd) – grandson, by Sadler's Wells
1996	Dushyantor (2nd) – grandson, by Sadler's Wells
	Shantou (3rd) – great-grandson, out of Shaima, by Shareef Dancer
1997	Silver Patriarch (2nd) – great-grandson, by Saddler's Hall, by Sadler's Wells
	Romanov (3rd) – grandson, by Nureyev
1998	City Honours (2nd) great-grandson, out of Ikebana, by Sadler's Wells

IRISH DERBY

1970	Nijinsky
1977	The Minstrel

1981	Dance Bid (3rd)
1982	Assert – grandson, by Be My Guest
1983	Shareef Dancer
	Caerleon (2nd) – grandson, by Nijinsky II
1984	El Gran Senor
1986	Shahrastani – grandson, by Nijinsky II
	Bakharoff (3rd) – grandson, by The Minstrel
1988	Kahyasi – great-grandson by Ile de Bourbon by Nijinsky II
1989	Old Vic – grandson, by Sadler's Wells
	Ile de Nisky (3rd) – great-grandson, by Ile de Bourbon by Nijinsky II
1990	Salsabil – granddaughter, by Sadler's Wells
	Belmez (3rd) – grandson, by El Gran Senor
1991	Generous – great-grandson, by Caerleon by Nijinsky II
	Suave Dancer (2nd) – great-grandson, by Green Dancer by Nijinsky II
	Star of Gdansk (3rd) – great-grandson, by Danzig Connection by Danzig
1992	St Jovite – great-grandson, out of Northern Sunset by Northfields
	Dr Devious (2nd) – great-grandson, out of Rose of Jerico out of Rose Red
1993	Commander-in-Chief – great-grandson, by Dancing Brave by Lyphard
	Hernando (2nd) – great-grandson, by Niniski by Nijinsky II
1994	Balanchine – granddaughter, by Storm Bird
	King's Theatre (2nd) – grandson, by Sadler's Wells
	Colonel Collins (3rd) – grandson, by El Gran Senor
1995	Winged Love – great-grandson, by In The Wings, by Sadler's Wells
1996	Zagreb – great-grandson, by Theatrical, by Nureyev
	Polaris Flight (2nd) – grandson, by Northern Flagship
	His Excellence (3rd) – grandson, by El Gran Senor
1997	Desert King – great-grandson, by Danehill, by Danzig. Out of Sabaah, by Nureyev
	Dr Johnson (2nd) – great-grandson, out of Russian Ballet, by Nijinsky II
	Loup Sauvage (3rd) – great-grandson, out of Louveterie, by Nureyev
1998	Dream Well – grandson, by Sadler's Wells, out of Soul Dream, out of Normia, by Northfields
	City Honours (2nd) – great-grandson, out of Ikebana, by Sadler's Wells
	Desert Fox (3rd) – grandson, by Sadler's Wells

PRIX DU JOCKEY-CLUB

1982	Assert – grandson, by Be My Guest
1983	Caerleon – grandson, by Nijinsky II
1984	Sadler's Wells (2nd)
1986	Bering – great-grandson, out of Beaune by Lyphard
	Bakharoff (2nd) – grandson, by The Minstrel
1987	Trempolino (2nd) – great-grandson, out of Trephine by Viceregal
1988	Ghost Busters (2nd) – great-grandson, out of Diala by Viceregal
1989	Old Vic – grandson, by Sadler's Wells
	Dancehall (2nd) – great-grandson, by Assert by Be My Guest
1991	Suave Dancer – great-grandson, by Green Dancer by Nijinsky 11
1993	Hernando – great-grandson, by Niniski, by Nijinsky II. Out of Whakilyric, out of Lyrism, by Lyphard

Dernier Empereur (2nd) by Trempolino out of Trephine by Viceregal
Hunting Hawk (3rd) – grandson, by Sadler's Wells
1994   Celtic Arms – great-grandson, out of Celtique by Northfields
Solid Illusion (2nd) – great-grandson, by Green Dancer by Nijinsky II
1995   Poliglote (2nd) – grandson, by Sadler's Wells
Winged Love (3rd) – great-grandson, by In The Wings, by Sadler's Wells
1996   Polaris Flight (2nd) – grandson, by Northern Flagship
1997   Peintre Célèbre – grandson, by Nureyev
Oscar (2nd) grandson, by Sadler's Wells
1998   Dream Well – grandson, by Sadler's Wells, out of Soul Dream, out of Normia, by Northfields
Sestino (3rd) – great-grandson, out of Stellina, by Caerleon, by Nijinsky II

KENTUCKY DERBY

1964   Northern Dancer
1984   Coax Me Chad (2nd) – great-grandson, by L'Enjoleur, out of Franfreluche
At The Threshold (3rd) – great-great-grandson, by Norcliffe, out of Drama School, by Lyphard
1985   Stephan's Odyssey (2nd) – grandson, by Danzig
Chief's Crown (3rd) – grandson, by Danzig
1986   Ferdinand – grandson, by Nijinsky II
1991   Mane Minister (3rd) – great-grandson, by Deputy Minister by Vice Regent
1992   Lil E Tee – great-great-grandson, by At The Threshold by Norcliffe out of Drama School
1993   Sea Hero – great-grandson, by Polish Navy by Danzig
1994   Strodes Creek (2nd) – great-grandson, out of Bottle Top by Topsider
1995   Thunder Gulch – great-grandson, out of Line of Thunder, by Storm Bird
Tejano Run (2nd) – great-great-great-grandson, out of Kazadancoa, by Green Dancer, by Nijinsky II
1996   Cavonnier (2nd) – great-grandson, out of Direwarning, out of Mazurka
Prince of Thieves (3rd) – great-great-grandson, by Hansel, out of Count on Bonnie, by Dancing Count
1997   Captain Bodgit (2nd) – great-great-grandson, out of Answering Echo, by Greek Answer, by Northern Answer
1998   Victory Gallop (2nd) – great-grandson, out of Victorious Lil, by Vice Regent
Indian Charlie (3rd) – great-great-grandson, out of Soviet Sojourn, by Leo Castelli, by Sovereign Dancer

Breeders' Cup

BREEDERS' CUP SPRINT

1984   Eillo – grandson, out of Barb's Dancer
1989   Dancing Spree – grandson, by Nijinsky II
1990   Dayjur (2nd) – grandson, by Danzig
1991   Sheikh Albadou – great-grandson, by Green Desert by Danzig
1992   Rubiano (3rd) – great-grandson, out of Ruby Slippers by Nijinsky 11
1993   Cardmania – great-great-grandson, out of L'Orangerie out of Liska by Lyphard
1994   Soviet Problem (2nd) – great-granddaughter, by Moscow Ballet by Nijinsky II
      Cardmania (3rd) – great-great-grandson, out of L'Orangerie out of Liska by Lyphard
1995   Desert Stormer – great-grandson, by Storm Cat, by Storm Bird
      Lit de Justice (2nd) – grandson, by El Gran Senor
1996   Lit de Justice – grandson, by El Gran Senor
      Honour and Glory (3rd) – great-great-grandson, out of Fair To All, by Al Nasar by Lyphard
1998   Reraise – grandson, by Danzatore
      Grand Slam (2nd) – great-grandson, out of Bright Candles by El Gran Senor

BREEDERS' CUP JUVENILE FILLIES

1987   Jeanne Jones (2nd) – granddaughter, by Nijinsky II
1988   Open Mind – great-granddaughter, by Deputy Minister by Vice Regent
      Lea Lucinda (3rd) – granddaughter, by Secreto
1989   Go For Wand – great-granddaughter, by Deputy Minister by Vice Regent
1990   Dance Smartly (3rd) – granddaughter, by Danzig
1993   Sardula (2nd) – great-granddaughter, by Storm Cat by Storm Bird
      Heavenly Prize (3rd) – great-granddaughter, out of Oh What A Dance by Nijinsky II
1994   Flanders – great-granddaughter, out of Starlet Storm by Storm Bird
      Serena's Song (2nd) – great-granddaughter, out of Imagining by Northfields
1995   Cara Rafaela (2nd) – great-granddaughter, out of Oil Fable out of Northern Fable
1996   Storm Song – great-granddaughter, by Summer Squall, by Storm Bird. Out

of Hum Along, out of Minstress, by The Minstrel
Love That Jazz (2nd) – granddaughter, by Dixieland Band

1997   Countess Diana – great-granddaughter, by Deerhound, by Danzig. Out of
        TV Countess, out of Count on Cathy, by Dancing Count
        Career Collection (2nd) – great-great-granddaughter, by General Meeting,
        out of Alydar's Promise, out of Summertime Promise, by Nijinsky II
        Primaly (3rd) – great-granddaughter, by Alydeed, by Shadeed, by
        Nijinsky II

1998   Silverbulletday – great-great-granddaughter, by Silver Deputy, by Deputy
        Minister, by Vice Regent
        Excellent Meeting (2nd) – great-great-granddaughter, out of Fitted Crown,
        by Chief's Crown, by Danzig

BREEDERS' CUP DISTAFF

1989   Open Mind – great-granddaughter, by Deputy Minister by Vice Regent
1990   Valay Maid (3rd) – granddaughter, by Carnivalay
1991   Dance Smartly – granddaughter, by Danzig
        Versailles Treaty (2nd) – granddaughter, by Danzig
1992   Versailles Treaty (2nd) – granddaughter, by Danzig
        Magical Maiden (3rd) – great-granddaughter, out of Gil's Magic by
        Magisterial
1994   Heavenly Prize (2nd) – great-granddaughter, out of Oh What A Dance by
        Nijinsky II
1995   Heavenly Prize (2nd) – great-granddaughter, out of Oh What A Dance, by
        Nijinsky II
1996   Serena's Song (2nd) – great-granddaughter, out of Imagining, by Northfields
        Different (3rd) – great-granddaughter, by Candy Stripes, out of Bubble
        Company, by Lyphard
1997   Ajina – great-great-granddaughter, by Strawberry Road, by Whiskey Road,
        by Nijinsky II
        Sharp Cat (2nd) – great-granddaughter, by Storm Cat, by Storm Bird
        Escena (3rd) – great-great-granddaughter, by Strawberry Road, by Whiskey
        Road, by Nijinsky II
1998   Escena – great-great-granddaughter, by Strawberry Road, by Whiskey Road,
        by Nijinsky 11
        Keeper Hill (3rd) – great-granddaughter, by Deputy Minister, by Vice
        Regent. Out of Fineza by Leopheor, by Lyphard

BREEDERS' CUP MILE

1984   Royal Heroine – great-granddaughter, by Lypheor by Lyphard
1985   Shadeed (3rd) – grandson, by Nijinsky II
1986   Last Tycoon – grandson, by Try My Best
        Palace Music (2nd) – grandson, by The Minstrel
        Fred Astaire (3rd) – grandson, by Nijinsky II
1987   Mièsque – granddaughter, by Nureyev
        Show Dancer (2nd) – grandson, by Sovereign Dancer

	Sonic Lady (3rd) – granddaughter, by Nureyev
1988	Mièsque – granddaughter, by Nureyev
1989	Most Welcome (3rd) – grandson, by Be My Guest
1990	Royal Academy – grandson, by Nijinsky II

Sonic Lady (3rd) – granddaughter, by Nureyev
1988 Mièsque – granddaughter, by Nureyev
1989 Most Welcome (3rd) – grandson, by Be My Guest
1990 Royal Academy – grandson, by Nijinsky II
    Itsallgreektome (2nd) – grandson, by Sovereign Dancer
    Priolo (3rd) – grandson by Sovereign Dancer
1991 Opening Verse – grandson, by The Minstrel
    Val des Bois (2nd) – great-grandson by Bellypha, by Lyphard
1992 Lure – grandson, by Danzig
    Paradise Creek (2nd) – great-grandson, out of North Of Eden by Northfields
1993 Lure – grandson, by Danzig
    Ski Paradise (2nd) – granddaughter, by Lyphard
    Fourstars Allstar (3rd) – grandson, by Compliance
1994 Barathea – grandson, by Sadler's Wells
    Johann Quatz (2nd) – grandson, by Sadler's Wells. Out of Whakilyric, out of Lyrism
    Unfinished Symph (3rd) – great-great-grandson, out of Accuwoman by Akureyri out of Royal Statute
1995 Sayyedati (3rd) – great-grandson, by Shadeed, by Nijinsky II
1996 Spinning World (2nd) – grandson, by Nureyev. Out of Imperfect Circle, out of Aviance, by Northfields
    Same Old Wish (3rd) – great-grandson, by Lyphard's Wish, by Lyphard
1997 Spinning World – grandson, by Nureyev. Out of Imperfect Circle, out of Aviance, by Northfields
    Geri (2nd) – great-grandson, by Theatrical, by Nureyev. Out of Garimperio, out of Far Flying, by Far North
    Decorated Hero (3rd) – great-grandson, out of Bequeath, by Lyphard
1998 Hawksley Hill (2nd) – great-great-grandson, out of Gaijin, by Caerleon, by Nijinsky II

BREEDERS' CUP JUVENILE

1984 Chief's Crown – grandson, by Danzig
1985 Storm Cat (2nd) – grandson, by Storm Bird
    Scat Dancer (3rd) – grandson, by Sovereign Dancer
1986 Qualify (2nd) – grandson, by Danzig
1987 Regal Classic (2nd) – grandson, by Vice Regent
1988 Tagel (3rd) – great-grandson, out of Featherhill by Lyphard
1989 Rhythm – grandson, out of Dance Number
    Grand Canyon (2nd) – great-great-grandson, out of Champagne Ginny by L'Enjoleur out of Fanfreluche
    Slavic (3rd) – grandson, by Danzig
1991 Arazi – grandson, out of Danseur Fabuleux
1992 River Special 3rd) – great-grandson, out of Nijinska Street by Nijinsky II
1993 Tabasco Cat (3rd) – great-grandson, by Storm Cat by Storm Bird
1994 Eltish (2nd) – great-grandson, out of Nimble Feet by Danzig
    Tejano, Run (3rd) – great-great-great grandson, out of Royal Run out of Cassadan Coa by Green Dancer by Nijinsky II
1995 Hennessy (2nd) – great-grandson, by Storm Cat, by Storm Bird

1996   Boston Harbour – great-grandson, out of Harbour Springs, by Vice Regent

Acceptable (2nd) – great-great-great-grandson, out of Ms Teak Wood, out of Willamae, out of Raclette, out of Laurie's Dancer

Ordway (3rd) – great-great-grandson, by Salt Lake, by Deputy Minister, by Vice Regent

1997   Nationalore (3rd) – great-great-grandson, by Video Ranger, out of Vestris, by Nijinsky II

1998   Answer Lively – great-great-grandson, out of Twosies Answer, out of Lady's Answer

Aly's Answer (2nd) – great-grandson, by Alwuhush, by Nureyev

Cat Thief (3rd) – great-grandson, by Storm Cat, by Storm Bird

BREEDERS' CUP TURF

1984   Raami (3rd) – grandson, by Be My Guest

1985   Strawberry Road (2nd) – great-grandson, by Whiskey Road, by Nijinsky II

1986   Manila – grandson, by Lyphard

Theatrical (2nd) – grandson, by Nureyev

1987   Theatrical – grandson, by Nureyev

Trempolino (2nd) – great-grandson, out of Trephine by Viceregal

1988   Indian Skimmer (3rd) – granddaughter, by Storm Bird

1990   In The Wings – grandson, by Sadler's Wells

With Approval (2nd) – great-grandson, out of Passing Mood out of Cool Mood

1991   Itsallgreektome (2nd) – grandson, by Sovereign Dancer

Quest For Fame (3rd) – great-great-grandson, out of Aryene by Green Dancer by Nijinsky II

1992   Sky Classic (2nd) – grandson, by Nijinsky II

Quest For Fame (3rd) – great-great-grandson, out of Aryenne by Green Dancer by Nijinsky II

Fraise – great-great-grandson – by Strawberry Road, by Whiskey Road, by Nijinsky II

1993   Kotashaan – great-great-great-grandson, out of Haute Autorite out of Première Danseuse by Green Dancer by Nijinsky II

Bien Bien (2nd) – great-great-grandson, by Manila by Lyphard

1994   Hatoof (2nd) – great-granddaughter, out of Cadeaux d'Amie by Lyphard

Paradise Creek (3rd) – great-grandson, out of North Of Eden by Northfields

1995   Northern Spur – grandson by Sadler's Wells

Freedom Cry (2nd) – great-grandson, by Soviet Star, by Nureyev. Out of Falling Star, out of Free French

Carnegie (3rd) – grandson, by Sadler's Wells

1996   Pilsudski – great-grandson, by Polish Precedent, by Danzig

Singspiel (2nd) – great-grandson, by In The Wings, by Sadler's Wells

1997   Chief Bearhart – great-grandson, by Chief's Crown, by Danzig

Flag Down (3rd) – great-grandson, by Deputy Minister, by Vice Regent

1998   Buck's Boy – great-grandson, by Bucksplasher, out of Victoria Star

Yagli (2nd) – great-grandson, out of Nijinsky's Best, by Nijinsky

Dushyantor (3rd) – grandson, by Sadler's Wells

BREEDERS' CUP CLASSIC

1984	Gate Dancer (3rd) – grandson, by Sovereign Dancer
1985	Gate Dancer (2nd) – grandson, by Sovereign Dancer
1986	Ferdinand – grandson, by Nijinsky II
1992	Jolypha (3rd) – granddaughter, by Lyphard
1994	Tabasco Cat (2nd) – great-grandson, by Storm Cat by Storm Bird
	Dramatic Gold (3rd) – great-grandson, out of American Drama by Danzig
1995	Cigar – great-grandson, by Palace Music, by The Minstrel
	L'Carriere (2nd) – great-grandson, out of Northern Sunset, by Northfields
	Unaccounted For (3rd) – great-grandson, out of Mrs Jenny, by The Minstrel
1996	Louis Quatorze (2nd) – grandson, by Sovereign Dancer
	Cigar (3rd) – great-grandson, by Palace Music, by The Minstrel
1997	Deputy Commander (2nd) – great-grandson, by Deputy Minister, by Vice Regent
	Dowty (3rd) – great-grandson, out of Miss Carlotita, by Masqued Dancer, by Nijinsky II
1998	Awesome Again – great-grandson, by Deputy Minister, by Vice Regent

Northern Dancer's Stud Fees

YEAR	FEE ($)	TERMS
1965	10,000	live foal
1966	10,000	live foal
1967	10,000	live foal
1968	10,000	live foal
– moved to Maryland –		
1969	15,000	live foal
1970	15,000	live foal
1971	25,000	live foal
1972	25,000	live foal
1973	25,000	live foal
1974	25,000	live foal
1975	35,000	$10,000 non-refundable
1976	35,000	$10,000 non-refundable
1977	35,000	$10,000 non-refundable
1978	50,000	no guarantee
1979	50,000	no guarantee
1980	100,000	no guarantee
1981	150,000	no guarantee
1982	250,000	no guarantee
1983	300,000	no guarantee
1984	500,000	no guarantee

Thereafter until Northern Dancer retired from stud on 15 April 1987, as much as $1 million was paid for a single breeding with no guarantee.

Acknowledgements

Just as serendipity and curious turns of fate played a significant role in the saga of Northern Dancer, so these elements affected the creation of this book.

The idea to write it came to me on a sunny afternoon at Woodbine in June 1990. Between races I dropped into the book and gift shop with copies of *E.P. Taylor: A Horseman and His Horses* that the manager, Ursula Shutte, had ordered. Moments before I arrived, Ursula announced, a gentleman had left the shop disappointed that there were no books about Northern Dancer.

Ursula dragged me over to the bookshelves. 'Look,' she said. 'There – Secretariat. Two books on Nijinsky. It's ridiculous! There is not one book about Northern Dancer! And people keep asking for one. Why don't you write it?'

'Okay,' said I. It was that simple.

I was overjoyed and spent the rest of the afternoon grinning like someone who had bet the winners of the first six races. So, to the gentleman who asked for this book and Ursula for suggesting I write it, thanks.

That autumn I drove to Maryland to see Northern Dancer, as it would turn out, for the last time. While I was there I had planned to interview several people who, for various reasons, were now unavailable. I'd like to thank them for *not* being there, for they left me no option but to focus solely on Northern Dancer. I also wish to express my gratitude to Northern Dancer for demanding that I listen to him.

Dorothy Gail Chambers, neighbour, writer and Northern Dancer fan, volunteered to make the Maryland journey with my Jack Russell terrier and me. We had been waiting for more than an hour for Northern Dancer to leave his paddock, and a seafood lunch in nearby Chesapeake City was becoming increasingly attractive. Had my neighbour not insisted that we wait for Northern Dancer, I would have missed his rearing and screaming, and this would have been a different book. Thank you, Dorothy Gail.

I also wish to thank Northern Dancer's human family, Judith Mappin and Charles Taylor. Generous in their support, memories, and friendship, they read many drafts of the manuscript as it developed. Although this is not an official biography, they always offered valuable commentary, constructive criticism and encouragement.

Northern Dancer was a national hero. I knew this was meant to be a book for everyone who had been touched by him – not only those involved in thoroughbred sport – but I wasn't certain how to get there. When my editor, Charis Wahl, strolled in, it was like Rae 'le Crocodile' Johnstone and Nearctic. Charis was exactly what this book needed. Her contributions are beyond measure.

Right from the beginning Kate Wilson's publishing expertise, advice, technical suggestions and friendship were significant in guiding an idea into a finished book.

When the final draft of the manuscript was complete it went to Saskia and Gord Rowley at Beach Graphics. Their enthusiasm for *Northern Dancer* and its appearance is evident throughout their design.

While *Northern Dancer* certainly has been a labour of love, it took far longer to complete than I had originally planned. When I became discouraged, the horses – Northern Dancer, Nijinsky, The Minstrel, and the rest – lifted my spirits. It was impossible to write about these extraordinary animals without being affected by their brilliance and courage.

Whatever I needed to complete this book magically appeared. So many people graciously offered their time, memories, scrapbooks, photographs, reference books, insights and support. I'd specifically like to thank Michael Armstrong, David Vaughan and Gary Loschke, executive director of the Jockey Club of Canada. When some research or statistical detail eluded me, one or another of these men cheerfully helped get me back on course.

Other contributions include those of Bert Alexandra, Rick

Basciano, George Blackwell, André Blaetler, Jim Boylen, Bob Careless of the Ontario Jockey Club, Jenny Dereham, Trent Frayne, Beth Heriot, Jean Hills, Dr John Howard, Bill Husfelt, Annie Lennox, Elvin Letchford, Pierre Levésque, Charles Mappin, Pete McCann, Bernard McCormack, Virginia Oaks McKinney, Peter Poole, Wayne Reinsmith, Jim Rogers and the *Daily Racing Form*, Annie Stewart, Austin and Betsy Taylor, Ron Turcotte, Ric Waldman, Doris Warren of the Keeneland library and the staffs of Windfields and the other farms I visited.

The memory of three important mentors – of the times we spent and the conversations we shared – was so strong that I felt as if they were sitting next to me as I wrote. E.P Taylor taught me never to quit; Winifred Taylor reminded me to see the humour; and Harry Green showed me how to see the world through the eyes of a horse.

To my family and friends who dealt with my ecstasy when the book was going well and my misery when it wasn't – thanks for being there.

Finally I'd like to pay tribute to all the gallant thoroughbreds, the noblest creatures on this earth. They give all they have and ask for so little in return. We have much to learn from them.

Sources and References

Baerlein, Richard. *Nijinsky: Triple Crown Winner*. London: Pelham Books, 1971.

Coleman, Jim. *A Hoofprint on My Heart*. Toronto: McClelland and Stewart, 1971.

David, Roy. *Robert Sangster, Tycoon of the Turf*. London: William Heinemann Ltd., 1991.

Della Rochetta, Mario Incisa. *The Tesios As I Knew Them*. London: J.A. Allen, 1979.

Frayne, Trent. *Northern Dancer and Friends*. New York: Funk & Wagnalls, 1969.

The Queen's Plate. Toronto: McClelland and Stewart, 1959.

Graham, Clive. *Hyperion*. London: J.A. Allen, 1967.

Herbert, Ivor (advisory editor). *Horse Racing: The Complete Guide to the World of the Turf*. London: William Collins & Son, 1980.

Hirsch, Joe. 'The Grand Señor: The Fabulous Career of Horatio Luro.' Lexington: *Blood-Horse*, 1989.

Longrigg, Roger. *The History of Horse Racing*. New York: Stein & Day, 1972.

Robertson, William H.P. *The History of Thoroughbred Racing in North America*. Englewood Cliffs, N.J. Prentice Hall, 1964.

Shoemaker, Bill and Barney Nagler. *Shoemaker: America's Greatest Jockey*. New York: Doubleday, 1988.

Smith, Raymond. *Vincent O'Brien: The Master of Ballydoyle*. London: Virgin Books, 1990.

Tesio, Federico. *Breeding the Racehorse*. London: J.A. Allen, 1958.

Turcotte, Ron (with Bill Heller). *The Will to Win*. Saskatoon: Fifth House Publishers, 1992.

Varola, Franco. *The Tesio Myth*. London: J.A. Allen, 1984.

Newspapers and magazines:

I also read everything I could find that had been written about Northern Dancer and many of his offspring. I pored over hundreds of numbers of the *Blood-Horse*, *Daily Racing Form*, and *Thoroughbred Record* for valuable information. Other publications in the initial research included *Canadian Horse*, *The Globe and Mail*, *Herald and Leader*, *Horsemen's Journal*, *Maryland Horse*, *Pacemaker*, *Sports Illustrated*, *Spur*, *Thoroughbred Times*, *Toronto Star*, and *Toronto Telegram*.

Index